Irvin S. Cobb

Twayne's United States Authors Series

Kenneth E. Eble, Editor

University of Utah

TUSAS 493

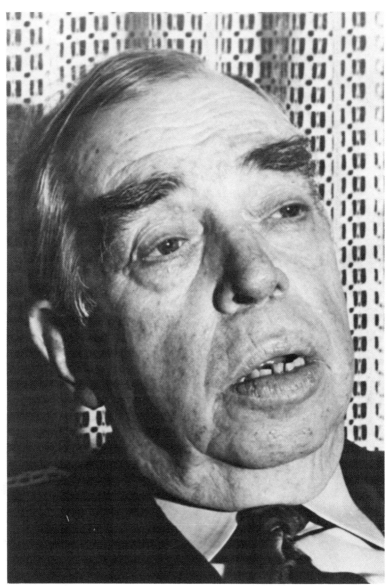

IRVIN S. COBB
(1886–1944)
Photograph courtesy of the
Paducah Public Library

Irvin S. Cobb

By Wayne Chatterton

Boise State University

Twayne Publishers • *Boston*

Irvin S. Cobb

Wayne Chatterton

Copyright © 1986 by G. K. Hall & Co.
All Rights Reserved
Published by Twayne Publishers
A Division of G. K. Hall & Co.
70 Lincoln Street
Boston, Massachusetts 02111

Copyediting supervised by Lewis DeSimone
Book production by Elizabeth Todesco
Book design by Barbara Anderson

Typeset in 11 pt. Garamond
by Compset, Inc. of Beverly, Massachusetts

Printed on permanent/durable acid-free paper
and bound in the United States of America

Library of Congress Cataloging in Publication Data

Chatterton, Wayne.
  Irvin S. Cobb.

  (Twayne's United States authors series)
  Bibliography: p. 148
  Includes index.
  1. Cobb, Irvin S. (Irvin Shrewsbury), 1876–1944— Criticism and interpretation.
  I. Title. II. Series.
PS3505.O14Z586   1986   818'.5209   85-17613
ISBN 0-8057-7452-1

To Andrew Halford and the People of Paducah
for making a Kentuckian out of a Rocky Mountaineer

Contents

About the Author

Born in Idaho and a lifetime resident of the Mountain West, Wayne Chatterton earned a Normal School Diploma and Teaching Certificate from Albion State Normal School in 1942. Thereafter he was awarded the B.A. and M.A. degrees in English literature and drama from Brigham Young University and the Ph.D. in English literature from the University of Utah. He has taught English and American literature and drama at Carbon Junior College, Southern Idaho College of Education, College of Idaho, and Boise State University. At present he is a professor emeritus of English and American literature at Boise State University.

In 1972, he originated the Western Writers Series at Boise State University and has served as coeditor of the series since that time. For this series he wrote the first booklet, *Vardis Fisher: The Frontier and Regional Works*. For the Twayne United States Authors Series he collaborated with Martha Heasley Cox in writing *Nelson Algren* (1975). He also wrote *Alexander Woollcott* (1978). He has written a Monarch Notes critical commentary and study guide for Nathanael West's *The Day of the Locust* (1978) and an article on the life and work of A. B. Guthrie, Jr., for the forthcoming *Literary History of the American West*.

Professor Chatterton served as a special lecturer in the American Studies Program at the College of Idaho and spent two terms as guest instructor in the American novel and drama at College of Idaho summer sessions in Sun Valley. He served four years as Idaho state director to the National Council of Teachers of English and three years as Idaho state chairman of the NCTE Achievement Awards.

Preface

For several years during the 1920s and 1930s, Irvin Cobb was the subject of daily discussions in the barber shops of America. I first heard of Cobb in a shop called the Star. It was my father's place of business and I was eight, perhaps nine years old. Growing up from hair-sweeper and spittoon polisher to shoe-shine boy, I listened hard and well.

People talked about everything in that shop, but what I remember best is the daily tangle of opinion over the latest "thing" by Cobb. For waiting customers the shop subscribed to the local papers and to such magazines as the *Saturday Evening Post*. So the latest "thing" was always there, to be passed around, waved in the air, or stabbed by a forefinger, depending upon what the speaker thought of the author at the moment.

On most days the barber-shop critics worked up a heated confrontation over whether Will Rogers or Cobb was funnier. The arguments were only opinions, of course, and everybody had a right to his own, so there was rarely a general settlement. If you liked short, homey stuff, written in language that "everybody talks" and that "hits the nail on the head," you would argue for Rogers. But if you would rather lean back and let the writer work up funny stuff that "sneaks up on you" and "tickles the old funny-bone," you would go for Cobb.

At bottom, these differences appear to have been the ones that mattered. In 1935, Rogers died in a plane crash and left the funny stuff to Cobb, who lived for another decade. But in the long run, Will's kind of humor has been remembered best. For whatever reason, American readers made their choice between the two most popular humorists of those years, and the nod went to Rogers.

As a result, Cobb's legacy to American humor has drifted from the awareness of most readers, who have never given themselves the opportunity to find out whether he has anything to offer them. Moreover, this drift has accelerated in almost direct proportion to the tenacious popularity of Rogers, which has deepened by the decade. However futile might be any suppositions that go contrary to real developments, one cannot altogether quash a feeling that Cobb would have been the leading humorist in any era save that of Mark Twain or Will Rogers and that in succeeding eras he might have been considered pretty much their equal.

The remarkable thing is that Cobb did not like to think of himself as a humorist. He did a great deal of work that was serious in nature and intent. He never poured more of himself into any pursuit than he did into the composition of the eerie fiction for which he was considered a master in his own time. Most important to him was the large amount of "straight reporting" he did, a form of writing he considered a time-honored craft and a high calling. Had his fame rested upon any of these serious forms, he would have felt better about his accomplishments than he did about the perverse label of "humorist" that stayed with him to the end of his days.

Only with reluctance did he accept that label, and in the broadness of his affections he could not think of Will Rogers as a rival. Cobb cherished his friendship with Rogers and never fully recovered from the private sense of loss that Will's premature and senseless death engendered in him.

The early chapters of this book explore the part that Paducah played in Cobb's life and in the formation of his talent as a writer. Herein, however, lies a problem for the critical biographer. The fact is that Cobb was a practicing and professional newspaperman when other young men of his age were still writing composition exercises in their high school English classes. During these years, indeed, he became the youngest editor of a daily paper in the United States, and by the time he was twenty-three he was writing his first important column, "Sourmash," for the *Louisville Evening Post*.

Throughout the forty-five years that followed "Sourmash," Cobb was a steady and tireless worker in almost every literary genre that was available to a writer of his time. He had learned his craft in the newspaper business, moreover, and had developed the habit of writing for "space rates." That is, he had found very early in his career that the amount of money in a paycheck frequently depended upon the amount of space he could legitimately fill with an article or column or story or whatever.

Given these early circumstances, Cobb had trained himself to get the most out of his subject in everything he wrote. In collected form, for instance, his short stories average nearly forty pages each, and if one considers that his short stories number in the hundreds, one can get some idea how voluminous his production is.

From Cobb's years in Paducah I have proceeded chronologically through his newspaper career and his transition to a literary career with the *Saturday Evening Post, Cosmopolitan,* and the publishing house of George Doran. Because it was as a humorist that Cobb made his earliest impression upon a broad readership, I have used chronology to trace the development of this aspect of his reputation.

With chapter 4, I give less importance to chronology and more to an examination of the nature of Cobb's humor. This emphasis leads to the Old Judge Priest tales and then to an exploration of the "folksy" and "back-yonder" ingredients in Cobb's work. In examining the Judge Priest stories, however, I have found it necessary to do a good deal of groundwork that has never been done before, particularly in unraveling the internal sequence and chronology of the stories, primarily from internal evidence. In so doing I have also been able to estimate the age of Judge Priest from the first story to the last and during crucial episodes between the extremes.

Thereafter, however, I leave matters of humor and other extensions of journalism in order to look at the "thriller" fiction for which, in his own time, he was almost as highly regarded. His last major work was a book that remains a triumph of autobiography, *Exit Laughing,* which by its nature and purpose returns us to the chronology of Cobb's career and takes us to the end of his days.

There are two old biographies of Cobb and one of recent vintage. Fred G. Neuman's *Irvin S. Cobb: His Life and Letters* (1938) was written by one of Cobb's friends from Paducah and is the nearest thing we have to an "authorized" biography. Writing almost in a tone of hero-worship, Neuman provides a treasure-trove of facts about Cobb's life and about the circumstances under which Cobb wrote almost everything he produced to 1938. Elisabeth Cobb's *My Wayward Parent* (1945) is honest, sprightly, and courageous, being at the same time an autobiography of the author and a biography of her famous father. In it, as nowhere else, one finds the private Irvin Cobb, who differs much from the public image. Anita Lawson's *Irvin S. Cobb* appeared while this manuscript was being edited and is currently the fullest, most objective, and best balanced biography of Cobb. For biographical material it is now the best source, particularly upon Cobb's work with motion pictures and upon his later years in general.

I have touched but lightly upon Cobb's career as Broadway playwright, as I have done upon his later years as movie scripter and actor for the Hal Roach studios. I have also done little with his western fiction. Besides these, he wrote a large amount of fiction that defies neat classification. In all of these areas there are stories of immense interest to any lover of good and ingenious fiction, though most of his short stories are overlong for the literary taste of our day.

I have not thoroughly discussed this material for two reasons. There is already a good deal of material about Cobb's life but no complete study of his writing, and in facing his voluminous writings, I have preferred to explore in some depth the three or four most important aspects of Cobb's literary career than to deal with many things superficially. Consequently, I have striven to write a thoroughgoing survey of those qualities of his writing for which Irvin S. Cobb deserves most to be remembered in the American literary pantheon.

Wayne Chatterton

Boise State University

Acknowledgments

To the writer of critical biography, acknowledgments of help are among the most perfunctory of tasks. But they are at the same time one of the most pleasant and satisfying of responsibilities. Without good and diligent librarians and other interested people, most books could not be written. Though I wish I could offer more, I take this opportunity to extend my gratitude to the following people and institutions:

Jacqueline Bull, special collections librarian, now retired, and Claire McCann, manuscript librarian and public services coordinator, for expert help and for permission to use material from the Irvin S. Cobb Papers, 1917–44, Special Collections and Archives, University of Kentucky Libraries.

Mrs. Doris Simon, librarian, and Tom Sutherland, director, Paducah Public Library, for permission to use material from the Irvin S. Cobb Collection.

Lois Cummings, serials clerk; Darryl Huskey, serials and documents librarian; Mrs. Ione Jolley and Miss Beverly Miller, interlibrary loan clerks, all of the Boise State University Library; also the Technical Review Committee at Boise State University for the awarding of a minigrant of $300 to help pay transportation for a research trip to the University of Kentucky at Lexington.

Helen Miller, Ardella Morrissey, and Kay Mushake of the Idaho State Library.

Miche Crane and Meriette Foreman, reference librarians at the Boise Public Library.

Andrew Halford, formerly chairman of the English Department, and Jenny Boyarski, librarian, Paducah Community College.

The people of Paducah, especially Mr. and Mrs. W. H. Beaman, directors of the Market House Museum; Miss Harriet Boswell, retired public librarian; John Pearce Campbell, Irvin Cobb's second cousin; Mrs. Elmer Ingram; Mrs. Bracket Owen of Owen's Island; Mr. Thomas Waller, the attorney who gave the memorial address at Cobb's funeral; Mr. Herbert Wallerstein, an old friend of Irvin Cobb; and Mrs. George Weicke.

Anne Kelly, instructor at the Pratt Institute Graduate School of Li-

brary and Information Sciences, and John A. White, student at the
Pratt Institute, for doing research with Cobb's special columns in the
New York Evening World and the *New York Sunday World*.

James H. Maguire, a colleague of mine in the English Department
at Boise State University, for his many valuable suggestions concerning
the manuscript.

Donald B. Smith, professor of history at the University of Calgary,
for sending his two articles on Cobb's good friend Buffalo Child Long
Lance.

Mrs. Jean Martin, librarian, Nampa (Idaho) High School, my willing and expert compiler of indexes.

My wife, Ardath, who is a better research assistant and amanuensis
than I deserve.

Chronology

Paths of Glory, Old Judge Priest, and *"Speaking of Operations."*

1916   "Under Sentence," *Fibble D. D., Speaking of Operations,* and *Local Color.*

1917–1918   *Speaking of Prussians, Those Times and These, The Glory of the Coming,* and *The Thunders of Silence.*

1919–1920   *The Life of the Party, From Place to Place, Eating in Two or Three Languages, The Abandoned Farmers,* and *Oh, Well, You Know How Women Are* in reply to M. R. Rinehart's *Isn't That Just Like a Man!*

1921   *A Plea for Old Cap Collier* and *One-Third Off.*

1922   *Jeff Poindexter, Colored* and *Sundry Accounts.* O. Henry Award for "Snake Doctor" as best short story of 1922. Begins ten-year stint as staff contributor to *Cosmopolitan.*

1923–1924   *Snake Doctor* and *A Laugh a Day.* Publishes eighty-eight stories in a 10-volume edition.

1925   *Here Comes the Bride* and *Many Laughs for Many Days.*

1926   *On An Island That Cost Twenty-four Dollars, Prose and Cons,* and *Some United States.*

1927–1928   *Chivalry Peak, Ladies and Gentlemen,* and *All Aboard.*

1929   *This Man's World, Irvin Cobb at His Best,* and *Red Likker.*

1930   *To Be Taken Before Sailing* and *Both Sides of the Street.*

1931   *Incredible Truth.*

1932   *Down Yonder with Judge Priest and Irvin S. Cobb.*

1933   *Murder Day by Day* and *One Way to Stop a Panic.* Radio debut on national network; continues programs twice a week.

1934–1935   *Faith, Hope and Charity.* Acts with Will Rogers in *Steamboat Round the Bend.*

1936   *Judge Priest Turns Detective.* On network radio for six months with a program called "Paducah Plantation."

1937   *Azam, The Story of an Arabian Colt and His Friends.* Movie, *Pepper.*

1938   Movie, *Hawaii Calls.*

1939   *Four Useful Pups.*

1941–1942   *Exit Laughing, Glory, Glory Hallelujah,* and *Roll Call.*

1944   *Curtain Call.* Cobb dies 10 March in New York of dropsy. Cremated, but ashes not interred until six months later on 7 October at Oak Park Cemetery in Paducah, Kentucky.

Chapter One

Never But One Paducah

Late in 1912, already famous as the creator of the "Old Judge Priest" stories and other tales, Irvin S. Cobb began paying his debt to Paducah. This little river town in western Kentucky was the home place of Cobb's birth and boyhood. Throughout his life he came back to Paducah again and again from his farthest wanderings over much of the globe. When he died, his ashes too were brought home to Paducah. They are buried in a grove of dogwood trees, and the site is marked by a large, rough-hewn boulder inscribed with the title of his first collection of local stories—"Back Home." In the preface to that collection, written in 1912, Cobb made this confession to his readers and to the people of Paducah: "For my material I draw upon the life of that community as I remembered it. Most of the characters that figure in the events hereinafter described were copies, to the best of my ability as copyist, of real models; and for some of the events themselves there was in the first place a fairly substantial basis of fact."[1]

Later in his career he was to say repeatedly that all his fiction had come from people he had known and from things he had seen and done. He must have intended his words to convey something uncommonly literal, for most of his stories contain characters that are easily recognizable composites of real people he had known, settings that are real places with real geographic names, and events that are often little changed from things that had happened to Cobb or to somebody he had known.

The clarity of detail that characterizes his fiction is a monument to that remarkable memory which astounded other writers with its accuracy, and which often seemed to them almost eerie in its comprehensiveness. Fully aware of the professional value of this asset, Cobb credited much of his success as a newsman to his capacity for remembering without written notes the sense, sequence, and language of any person he interviewed. He gave equal credit to what he called "an ability, first, mentally to photograph a scene or a person, and then to stow the picture away in a sort of filing system inside my head, where it stays properly catalogued and indexed against the time when I want to take it out and use it."[2] As the result of accurate self-assessment, Cobb later became aware that most of his short stories arose from memories of his "younger days."[3]

Most of the men who knew Cobb have spoken of this phenomenon. Many of these observers were themselves possessed of such learning and literary skill as to be impressed only by something prodigal in matters touching the craft of writing. To such people as these, Cobb's capacity to call up relevant yet sometimes bizarre information was both admirable and frustrating. His good friend and colleague O. O. McIntyre credited Cobb with being the most fruitful single source of ideas for his famous newspaper column, "New York Day by Day."[4] On the other hand, Cobb's crony and hunting companion, editor Robert H. Davis, once complained about the futility of anyone's trying to say anything that Cobb did not already know, with added detail and lengthy embellishment, from the plots and characters of books through quotations from the classic poets to the full-scale of American history and the science of ornithology. "Damn it," concludes Davis, "he knows everything."[5]

Among the things that Cobb remembered most clearly and most fully, among the things he felt most keenly and had assimilated most thoroughly, was the quality of life as the people of Paducah had lived it during his boyhood years in the 1880s and 1890s. To Paducahans, the best known and most accurate description of the town is a remark that Cobb made to a local interviewer during one of his frequent homecomings: "Here in Paducah one encounters, I claim, an agreeable blend of Western kindliness and Northern enterprise, superimposed upon a traditional Southern background."[6] Though in most ways Paducah was little different from thousands of other small towns all over America, its unique geographic location helped to create a correspondingly unique cultural aura and life-style for its inhabitants. To Cobb, during his boyhood years, the bustling little river town was like no other place in the habitable universe. Looking back from the perspective afforded him by global travel and the passage of many years, Cobb was to say repeatedly, "There never was but one Paducah; there never will be but one Paducah."[7]

Looking Back: The Usable Material of Boyhood

Despite its remoteness from sophisticated cultural areas and from centers of literary activity—the nearest was St. Louis, 150 miles north, up the Mississippi—the Paducah of Cobb's boyhood was a surprisingly fertile place for spawning a young writer. Though the community was small, with hardly more than 15,000 inhabitants, it had a long history for a town located so deep in the older "West."

Originally an attractive spot for the camps of explorers and fur traders coming down the Ohio to the Mississippi, Paducah was one of the first recognizable settlements inside the "Jackson Purchase" of 1818. The name "Paducah" became attached to the area in 1819, when Chickasaw tribesmen are said to have brought the remains of their legendary Chief Paduke to the site. They wanted to bury their chief in the ideal hunting ground.[8]

During Cobb's boyhood, the settlement was rich in historical heritage and Indian lore. Its cultural isolation was offset by the booming river traffic, which gave the town a sense of being very much a part of the great world to the east and north. Most important, the town had mellowed in the years since the frontier had passed it by, and it abounded in material attractive to a young writer's imagination. "A long-settled community with traditions behind it and a reasonable antiquity," wrote Cobb, "seems to breed curious types of men and women as a musty closet breeds mice and moths."[9]

Into these traditions and this antiquity, Irvin Shrewsbury Cobb was born on 23 June 1876. As for literary progenitors, on his father's side there were none worth mentioning, and on his mother's side only one or two appear to have anticipated in the blood line a first rate American humorist and fictioneer. In *Exit Laughing,* at the beginning of the chapter titled "This Business of Being a Descendant," Cobb declares his belief that "the fused and reconciled traits of his forebears form the core of the average man's character, and environment, generally speaking, is no more than the shellac which overlies these passed-on heritages" (*EL,* 18). Yet, in the genealogical tracings that Cobb commissioned as background for his autobiography, he found that his paternal grandparents came from Ireland and made their way in America mostly as iron-workers and foundrymen, keelboaters, owners and operators of river steamboats, and tobacco merchants. These were the family occupations all the way to "Josh" Cobb, who was Irvin's father.[10]

Among the Welsh antecedents on his mother's side, however, there was one James Saunders, Irvin's great-grandfather, who was known throughout his life as "Dry-Talkin' Jimmy" or, for handier use, "Jimmy Dry." Though born in Virginia during the Revolutionary War, and though apprenticed young to the tanning trade, "Jimmy Dry" Saunders took up a long rifle and followed the trail of his kinsmen to Kentucky. There he married a South Carolina girl, built a cabin near Frankfort, and settled down to raise a family and to perpetuate the nickname which he had earned by his "whimsical salty manner of speech" (*EL,* 28). One of his sons, Reuben Saunders, was apprenticed as a printer and bookbinder. But later he went to medical school, became world-famous for his discovery of atropine as a cure for cholera, and lived for many years as the leading general practitioner in Paducah. Save for the legendary wit and homespun humor of "Jimmy Dry," and save for the early training of Reuben Saunders as a bookbinder, nothing in Irvin Cobb's ancestry predicts or explains his own gifts for the journalistic and the literary.

In his loyalty to Kentucky, Cobb felt himself typical of all true Kentuckians, and he yielded nothing to the advocates of any other state, however fervent their arguments. "Being a Virginian is a profession, and being a South Carolinian is a trade to be worked at in season and out," wrote Cobb, "but Kentuckianism is an incurable disease, a disease, though, to be proud of" (*EL,* 18). Typical of this breed of native son, sharing its inordinate pride in the land of Daniel Boone and William Clark, Cobb became in many ways the purest symbol of the Kentuckian to whom the eastern hill country, the great central blue-grass, and the western river borders are all and equally Kentucky, however different the provincial culture and locale. To Irvin Cobb, there never was but one Paducah, and Paducah was also Kentucky.

At Paducah—the place that was to be forever his corner of Kentucky—Irvin Shrewsbury Cobb was born in the house of his maternal grandfather, the aforesaid Dr. Reuben Saunders, on South Third between Washington and Clark streets, within easy sight and chunk-chucking distance of the river's edge. In that "flat-faced, high-shouldered old house" (*EL,* 40) whose front windows looked across Third Street to the lip of the levee, only a block or two away, young Irvin spent the first nine years of his boyhood. Then he was removed to the place known as the "old Cobb home" near the middle of the present business district.

Within a few more years, at the age of sixteen, he was thrust prematurely into man's estate as a working member of the fourth estate. Like another small boy who grew up half a century earlier in a small riverbank town about three hundred miles north along the Mississippi, Irvin Cobb lived so rich a childhood and was so profoundly affected by the people he knew and the things he did that in the years of his literary fame there was some speculation about the possibility of his being considered the legitimate successor to Mark Twain.[11] At least one area of comparison is unmistakable: What Hannibal had been to Samuel Langhorne Clemens, Paducah was to Irvin Cobb.

Consecrated Reader: Classics versus Nickel Libraries

Cobb's formal schooling was remarkable for its brevity and for the successive alternations of private and public institutions to which his parents entrusted his intellectual development. At the age of seven he spent his first year of formal instruction in the private primary school of Miss Mary Gould, but he was then transferred to a public institution, the old Paducah Seminary, where he remained through the third grade. For reasons that have never been clear to anyone outside the family, Irvin's parents enrolled him once again in a private school maintained by Dr. Lewis Shuck in the old First Baptist Church building. He remained here through the fifth grade before he was returned to public instruction at Longfellow School. Here he went into the seventh grade and was allowed to skip the eighth in order to enter the ninth, which seemed more suitable to the level of his precocity in almost every academic area save the mathematical sciences, which were always beyond his comprehension. For two years after he finished the ninth grade, young Cobb sought private instruction again, this time at the academy maintained by Professor William A. Cade in an area of Paducah that came to be known as "Arcadia." But at this point in what seems a brilliant if erratic and lop-sided intellectual development, something cataclysmic happened within the family, and his formal schooling ended abruptly.

As Cobb himself preferred to explain the circumstances, "a sudden and disastrous shift in the family finances made it imperative for me to make my own living."[12] But what Irvin rather delicately called a shift in family finances was more likely the immediate result of his father's "starting a really spirited campaign to drink himself to death."[13] At any rate, it seemed to Irvin that the welfare of his family now depended entirely upon his willingness to become a full-time breadwinner.[14]

However tragic this event must have appeared to Irvin in the domestic sense, it diverted him from two alternative plans that would have deprived him of the early journalistic discipline upon which his career as a writer was to be founded. In this sense it was fortunate that he had to abandon the idea of going to military school as preparation for college, and that he could discover no immediate pecuniary advantage in the otherwise attractive prospect of studying law in a local office along "legal row."

His school days were clearly over by the time he was sixteen, and he knew that he must find some career for which, by education and personal preference, he appeared to be best suited. By one of the fortunate accidents of his lifetime, he found in the office of the local newspaper a career which he was to love and for which his brief schooling had given him surprisingly good preparation.

Reports from his various teachers abound in comments upon the quickness of his perceptions, the ease and rapidity with which he absorbed the content of reading matter, the accuracy and retentiveness of his memory, the originality of his viewpoints, and the ingenuity and effectiveness with which he marshaled ideas for exposition or argument. From the beginning of his schooling to its early end, however, young Irvin's tendency toward compulsive talking was a disruption to his classmates and a trial for his teachers. Moreover, his insatiable curiosity led him into more mischief than could easily be overlooked. For most of his teachers it was a moot question whether his promise as a student was adequate compensation for the spontaneous overflow of his conversation, or even whether his unusual talents in drawing and composition were worth the indignities that he wrought by his practical jokes.

For the satisfaction of working with a pupil whose love for reading was insatiable and whose comprehension seemed uncanny, however, young Irvin's teachers were willing to tolerate a great deal. Under the special attentions he flourished rapidly if somewhat at random in literature and history. To the bemusement of his teachers in the secondary grades, he asked questions sophisticated beyond the capacity of an ordinary teacher to give satisfactory answers. For these reasons, Irvin was fortunate in having free access to a wide variety of reading matter during his boyhood. In the Saunders home, where Irvin spent nearly the first ten years of his life, the library of his well informed grandfather was always open for his use and pleasure. It remained open to him until the old man died at the age of eighty-two. Moreover, the boy enjoyed the encouragement of "Uncle" Jo Shrewsbury, whose surname Irvin's parents had selected as the boy's middle name.

Whether for his success as a writer Irvin was more indebted to his grandfather Saunders or to "Uncle" Jo Shrewsbury is difficult to know.

In retrospect it has seemed to Cobb's daughter "Buff" that the taciturn old Dr. Saunders was the only member of the family who ever tried to plan for his favorite grandson's future, or who had the means to do so.[15] But the special rapport that Irvin enjoyed with "Uncle" Jo Shrewsbury—a relationship more cronylike than avuncular—did more than anything else to shape his cast of mind and heart toward the artistic and the literary. Between his sixth and his thirteenth year, by his own account, Irvin was "the faithful tagging shadow" (*EL,* 86) of "Uncle" Jo, who was not a blood relative but a close friend of the family, having been best man at "Josh" Cobb's wedding. Throughout their lives, until the moment of Josh's death, Jo remained an intimate friend.

To Irvin, Joel Shrewsbury became one of those informally adopted "uncles" who are frequently closer to children than are true kin, and whose influence upon the young is for that reason the greater. Among the boyhood things, "everlastingly inscribed on the tablets of my memory" (*EL,* 81), Cobb recounts many colorful events that he shared with his father and "Uncle" Jo and the local "waterfronters" on the porch of the riverside boat store at "Monkey Wrench Corner." With particular fondness he recalls how powerfully he was influenced by the crusty solicitudes of the old bachelor who, in Irvin's experience, remained unmatched "for eccentricities, for lovable whims and unaccountable crotchets, for a scalding tongue and a blistering pen and a self-kindling temper" (*EL,* 85).

At any rate, Irvin was willing to accept from "Uncle" Jo, if from no other person, the advice that a practical proficiency in Latin was one of the marks of a Southern gentleman, and he was willing to let "Uncle" Jo give him his first lessons in Latin grammar. Under tutorial arrangements which "Uncle" Jo made and paid for, Irvin also received his first training in the arts of music, dancing, and horsemanship. But having a "bad ear" he made only modest progress in music and the dance. Of his horsemanship he later remarked, "No matter what the horse does, I canter" (*EL,* 87).

Young Irvin was deeply and permanently impressed by "Uncle" Jo's capacity to converse in pure and formal language, to quote endlessly from the world's best literature, and, upon provocation, to shift into the richest and most picturesque of gutter language. "Uncle" Jo was able to sustain the latter level of communication until he had exhausted the standard vocabulary of contempt and vituperation, whereupon with unmatched ingenuity he invented his own. With equal facility, "Uncle" Jo wrote highly personalized articles of praise and abuse for the *Paducah Evening News,* and when Irvin was offered a job on that newspaper he remembered "Uncle" Jo's attempts to teach him journalism.

Between the respectable private library of his grandfather Saunders and the regular flow of carefully chosen if sometimes provocative reading matter that his "Uncle" Jo Shrewsbury pressed upon him, Irvin became acquainted early with most of the stock literary classics that were considered appropriate for juvenile reading. With the help of these sources he became acquainted also with a wide selection of reading matter that was well advanced for a boy of his years.[16] Throughout his life, Cobb confessed a special fondness for the first book that he read entirely on his own initiative—Stanley's *Adventures in Africa.* In this way he also met the works of Defoe, Scott, Cooper, Dickens, and Maupassant. Apart from the regular classroom samplings of Shakespeare, young Irvin was able to read many of the complete plays, copies of which were supplied by his two favorite mentors. Later in life he discovered that his early reading had given him a permanent fondness for the comedies.

One of the main reasons why Irvin Cobb became what may be called a "consecrated reader"[17] is that, despite his advanced proficiency in reading and his respect for the literary "classics," he was by no means a literary snob. To the discomfiture and disappointment of his elders, he soon became addicted to that species of subliterature known to his parents as the "dime novel" and known to his own generation as the "nickel library" (invariably pronounced *nickul librury*).

At home he read the Testaments and remembered the biblical tales so well that they were ready to his tongue and his pen as long as he lived. To learn proper Southern graciousness and hospitality, he read the works of Scott and the letters of Lord Chesterfield, as members of all good families were expected to do at that time. In school he was among the leaders of his class at going progressively through the graded selections of the McGuffey readers. More often than any of his classmates, therefore, he was called upon to recite poems of Arnold and Longfellow and all the other edifying writers whom the classroom texts offered for the emulation of generations. He became a true convert to the large-scale heroes and to the expansive and spectacular events in the novels of J. Fenimore Cooper.

But for his own private satisfaction he screened behind the pages of his open geography book the exciting frontier fictions of Ned Buntline and Mayne Reid, or the juvenile adventure tales of John Esten Cooke, or the broad local color and dialect humor of George Washington Harris' "Sut Lovingood." In the secrecy of the hayloft in the barn behind the Cobb home he spent infinitely more time with literature of this stamp and with such lively authors as Mark Twain and Robert Louis Stevenson, than with all the "deep literature" put together.

Long after Cobb's literary tastes had matured he looked back upon his boyhood reading habits, and more than half seriously he expressed his doubts whether a clear-headed youngster could have found the children's "classics" nearly as convincing and therefore nearly as meaningful as he had found those tales from the "nickul libruries." Just as Mark Twain had used "The Literary Offenses of Fenimore Cooper" to make a special form of high and biting humor out of the real if exaggerated weaknesses of Cooper, Cobb used *A Plea for Old Cap Collier* (1921) to evoke the same brand of humor from the real weaknesses of many perennial "classics" that were part of the old McGuffey readers.

In its own way, the humor of Cobb's mock-critical essay is as spontaneous and as full-blown as Twain's. But Cobb's underlying purpose is different from Twain's. To achieve that purpose, Cobb adds an extra dimension to the mockery. Both authors specialize in uncovering and holding up to the reader's view an egregious literary caricature of faults which every reader has noticed but has forced himself to accept under a "willing suspension of disbelief." Twain contents himself with tearing away the aesthetic veil that helps to screen Cooper from the ridicule of the purely logical critic, and he does so with a special quality of mock seriousness unmatched by any other American humorist save perhaps Irvin Cobb. The Kentuckian achieves the same quality of humor in his examination of such McGuffey "classics" as Scott's "Young Lochinvar" and Longfellow's "Excelsior."

But Cobb uses the critical analysis for an ulterior purpose: to demonstrate that, by comparison, the high adventure tales of Tombstone Dick, Redtop Rube, Kit Carson, and Old Cap Collier are actually more convincing and more truly moral and therefore more beneficial to the juvenile reader than the standard "classics" have been. He would give to his own son, he says, all the "nickul libruries" he could find, and would offer this advice: "Read them for their brisk and stirring movement; for the spirit of outdoor adventure and life which crowds them; for their swift but logical processions of sequences; for the phases of pioneer Americanism they rawly but graphically portray, and for their moral values."[18] Moreover, to overcome any scruples of taste that might prevent the tender and untried reader from adopting the right values,

Cobb offers this advice: "Never mind the crude style in which most of them are written. It can't be any worse than the stilted and artificial style in which your school reader is written."[19]

However outrageous this ebullient spoof of the children's school-room "classics" may seem, the underlying tone of Cobb's argument is sincere, at least where his own literary values are concerned. In developing his own style of writing, Cobb avoided all suggestion of the stilted and the artificial in favor of brisk movement and colloquial language.

The Romantic River

The short space between Cobb's tenth and his sixteenth years—the school years, when he still lived in the "old Cobb house"—spanned the only real boyhood he was to have, in the common sense of that word. For Cobb, these years are strongly reminiscent of the *Tom Sawyer* and *Huckleberry Finn* boyhood of his Missouri neighbor Mark Twain. Even more exhaustively than Twain, however, Cobb was to use the experiences of those years over and over again as the substance of his writing.

Like the young Twain, Irvin Cobb haunted the boat docks at the river's edge. For Cobb, the great Ohio River lay always only a few blocks away, at the foot of the main thoroughfares of the town. There, flowing in a wide, watery plain around Owen's Island, the Tennessee and the Ohio joined in their mutual journey to the Mississippi and the Gulf. With its waters open around the year, the Paducah river port enjoyed the continuous traffic of all the connected rivers. Moreover, Irvin's father worked at the principal boat house. There the boy heard all the news, all the gossip, all the lore of the rivers in the days when a good deal of romance was left in a long but fast-dying tradition of riverboating on the Southern waterways.

By the fortunate circumstance that Irvin Cobb was born at the right time and in the right place to be a part of the great days of riverboating before they passed forever, he remains the last gifted chronicler of one of the most colorful eras in American history and folklore. In Cobb's day, the magnificent antebellum river traffic of Twain's time had long been gone and could never be resurrected as Twain had known it. Along the Mississippi, the railroads had erased the romance of river-boating as Twain had seen that romance through a boy's eyes in *Tom Sawyer* and *Huckleberry Finn,* and as he had lived it as a pilot in *Life on the Mississippi.* But inland, along the great tributaries of the lower Mississippi, the rivers were still the principal means of travel and transportation all the way to and through Irvin Cobb's boyhood years.

From Paducah at its mouth to the end of its navigable waters at Chattanooga, the Tennessee River offered the only practical mode of heavy transportation for the dozens of riverbank hamlets along its way. For that reason the river traffic survived there almost into the 1930s, and though the modern craft were far less regal and colorful than were their forebears, Cobb observed that on the Tennessee in the late 1920s "there may yet be found the steamboating life, the steamboating adventures, the steamboating characters and types which almost have vanished elsewhere":[20]

On a single day in the flush years I've seen ten or twelve steamers, lordly deep-bellied sidewheelers and limber slender sternwheelers, ranked two or three abreast at the landing; and the inclined wharf, from the drydocks almost up to the marine ways, literally blocked off with merchandise incoming or freight outgoing—cotton in bales, tobacco in hogsheads, peanuts in sacks, whiskey in barrels and casks, produce and provender of a hundred sorts. Transfer boats and ferryboats and fussy tugs and perhaps a lighthouse tender or a government "snag boat" would be stirring about; both of the squatty scowlike wharf boats bulging with perishable stuffs; "coon-jining" rousters bearing incredible burdens and still able to sing under their loads, swearing mates and sweating "mud-clerks"; drays and wagons and hacks and herdics rattling up and down the slants; twin lanes of travelers dodging along the crowded gangplanks; a great canopy of coal smoke darkening the water front; a string band playing on the guards of some excursion steamer; . . . a calliope blasting away from the top of a visiting showboat (*EL,* 76)

Before Cobb was out of his teens, the railroads had come to the Kentucky river country, and Paducah was the divisional center for two major lines. As the railroads grew, the river traffic subsided, and with it went the major allied industries: tobacco, lumber, whiskey, mule and horse breeding, tanning and leather work, grist milling—all that had seemed colorful and distinctive during Cobb's boyhood years. But Cobb had known this life at first hand during his most impressionable years, when "the river either touched the lives or furnished the living for nearly every household" (*EL,* 75).

A Storyteller's Place, a Yarnspinner's People

Even more than most boys of his age, Irvin Cobb was a passionate collector. But he was not satisfied with the typical boyhood practice of collecting stamps and cigarette pictures, in which pursuit most of his playmates maintained a busy exchange among themselves.

Irvin's impressive collection of bird's eggs was a manifestation of his genuine interest in the natural sciences. As a result, his boyhood collections were the basis for a lifelong study of ornithology, a science in which he achieved considerable renown as an amateur naturalist. From the time when he built his boyhood herpetarium in the stable loft, he dated a lifelong interest in the peculiarities of reptiles, both indigenous and exotic. From time to time in his career as a writer he drew directly upon this intimate acquaintance of his boyhood, and he startled his readers with his knowledge of poisonous reptiles whose habits and appearance were essential to the verisimilitude of a story.

In the Indian burial mounds near Paducah, young Irvin found the artifacts that whetted his curiosity concerning the daily life of the local tribes. From his insatiable collecting of these artifacts he derived a larger interest in history and ethnology. Eventually this interest became part of his tireless urge to absorb all he could of the lore and folkways peculiar to the region.

Of all the collections he made as a young man in Paducah, his collection of Indian relics was the only one which he kept and built upon throughout his life. He was fond of studying the Indian tongues, of wearing Indian costumes in his home, of observing simple Indian customs, and of using Indian robes and utensils wherever they were practicable in his own life. Recognizing his deep respect for Indian customs, and acknowledging this sympathy with their way of life, the Blackfeet adopted him as a brother.

All the treasured artifacts of Irvin's boyhood collections remained bright and clear in his memory, even those he had laid away and lost. But none of them surpassed the lore of daily life in Paducah town, which furnished his recollections with a storehouse of sensations and experiences upon which he was to draw as a tale-teller. As a "spinner of yarns," he was to profit by his fascination with the life of the river and the waterfront, whose rich oral traditions had first taught him the lesson that "facts can be as outlandish as you please, but . . . fiction has to stick closer to what sounds plausible" (AA, 208). He was also to remember with uncommon vividness all the sensations that besieged him as he wandered the streets and byways of the town. He recalled how easily he, or anybody, could tell the part of town by its distinctive odor: "the almost suffocating rankness of the heavy fire-cured weed [tobacco] . . . the lovely savor from the stacks of fresh-cut lumber and mountain ranges of moist sawdust . . . the heavy alcoholic reek of 'Whiskey Row' on Market Street; the all pervading ammoniacal scent that rose off the wagon yards and mule-trading pens" (*EL,* 75).

The town had its feuding families, "not one of those sanguinary feuds of the mountains, involving a whole district, . . . nor yet a feud handed down as a deadly legacy from one generation to another until its origin is forgotten . . . but a shabby, small neighborhood vendetta affecting two families only."[21] In a town so busy and yet so villagelike, all personal misfortune became public knowledge. In a tone of wry compassion, Cobb wrote that "we had our tragedies that endured for years and, in the small-town way, finally became institutions."[22] Moreover, as might be expected, all such private affairs became general knowledge through "the small-town gossip of the small town."[23]

But the town was often festive, too. Besides its fervent political rallies and the standard patriotic holidays, the town had its circus days, when the whole populace turned out at dawn to watch the elephants and the roustabouts unload the railroad cars. Unlike other towns, Paducah had Josh Cobb, Irvin's father, who was possessed of a compulsion to gather up all the children he could find and take them to the afternoon performance. These were happy occasions, in whose memory Irvin wrote, "If there is any of the boy-spirit left in us circus day may be esteemed to bring it out."[24]

As the lone considerable settlement in the southern and western tip of the only state to declare an armed neutrality during the Civil War, Paducah enjoyed peculiarities of behavior and attitude that made this town seem different from other small towns in America during Cobb's adolescent years. All through the Reconstruction, the Kentuckians had proved themselves to be primarily Kentuckians "rather than Union Nationalists or Southern Irreconcilables."[25] Most Paducahans, however, retained the almost rabid Southern sentiment which had sent most of its men into the Confederate ranks.

The result was that, though most of Kentucky remained truly split in its allegiances, with considerable Northern sympathy in the population centers northeastward along the Ohio, the Paducah veterans were often more fiercely Confederate than were those veterans from towns deep in the South. As late as the 1890s, when young Irvin sat on the porch of Judge Bishop's house and listened to the oldsters spin their yarns, "a stranger might have been pardoned for supposing that

it was only the year before, or at most two years before, when the
Yankees came through under Grant; while Forrest's raid was spoken of
as though it had taken place within the current month."[26]

The unique blending of attitudes from the Northern, Southern, and
Western regions of the United States created an unusual relationship
between the black and white people of Paducah. In this community
the social structure had only superficially incorporated the typical
Southern interactions between the black populace and the white. As a
hometown boy, Irvin Cobb felt keenly and was therefore able to depict
with extraordinary accuracy the complex and sometimes almost mystic
subtleties by which the perfectly understandable "color line" of a
Northern and Western border state allowed its black and white residents to maintain a friendship, a respect, and sometimes a devotion for
each other, even while they also kept an inviolable distance between
the races on both sides.

Out of Cobb's appreciation of these subtleties comes the incomparable fictional character of Jefferson Poindexter, colored. And out of
Cobb's sympathetic awareness of these complexities comes the devotion
that prevails indissolubly between Jeff Poindexter and Old Judge
Priest. Out of this awareness come also the vivid tales that depict the
precarious subtleties whereby Jeff and the other "darkies" of the community manage their own affairs and whereby they keep their private
things to themselves. By Cobb's perceptions this was a race so secretive
that no white person at that time could hope to understand truly the
thoughts and feelings of even the closest among his black friends.
"Show me the white man who claims to know intimately the working
of his black servant's mind, who professes to be able to tell anything
of any negro's lodge affiliations or social habits or private affairs," wrote
Cobb, "and I will show you a born liar."[27] Yet so deep was Irvin's
affection for an old family servant that he dedicated *Those Times and
These* (1917) as follows: "to the memory of MANDY MARTIN, whose soul
was as white as her skin was black, and who for forty-two years, until
her death, was a loyal friend and servant of my people."

Long Pants and Fauntleroy Suits

In all of Cobb's reminiscences of his boyhood in Paducah, and in all
of the stories that are based upon his boyhood experiences, there is a
motif of increasing perspective and social awareness. In some respects
it is a boyhood that hearkens back to the Tom Sawyer world of Mark

Twain nearly half a century earlier. It is a fictional world of eternal boyhood, full of the arcana, the mystic rites, the misadventures, and the egregious disobediences of adolescents to whom adulthood is a foreign realm. Save in purely romantic daydreams, the boys and girls do not believe that they can penetrate the grown-up world, or that they ever will.[28] But by the last decade of the century, the social fiber of the frontier river towns appears to have become perceptibly more refined, and in the boyhood world of Cobb's fiction there is a hint of greater sophistication, an awareness among the young people that they are in a continual process of becoming adults.

As in the *Penrod* cycle of Booth Tarkington (begun in 1913), little boys are mostly little boys, but as they grow they must learn to be young men or "little gentlemen," and sometimes they are not sure which they are supposed to be. In any event, all such transitions are embarrassing and painful, especially in matters of dress and manners. Just as Tarkington's Penrod Schofield eventually reaches that early phase of social awareness when "for the first time in his life he knew the wish to be sand-papered, waxed and polished to the highest possible degree,"[29] Irvin Cobb looked forward with nearly unbearable anticipation to the moment when he could put on his first pair of long pants. With this simple but symbolic act, "he was a different person and it was a different world."[30]

In terms of the outlandish costumes which a boy might have to wear before he reached this rite of passage, no enormity of the period could surpass the "Little Lord Fauntleroy" suit. These were the years when the Little Lord Fauntleroy suit (inspired by Frances Hodgson Burnett's novels) had infected "thousands of the worthy matrons of America with a catching lunacy which raged like a sedge-fire, . . . and left enduring scars upon the seared memories of its chief sufferers."[31] During this era, a boy was unfortunate to be a "pretty child," since his mother was almost certain to "make him wear his hair long and force him to go about in public in a broad lace collar and a black velvet suit with a sash about his waist, and that means other boys will call him by offensively apt nicknames and generally make his life a burden to him."[32] Cobb's narrative of one such sufferer is an amusing chapter titled "Little Lord Pantsleroy" in *Goin' on Fourteen* (1924). The adolescent hero of this book is Juney Custer, who "has seemed to many critics as lovable and thoroughly human a creation as has graced the pages of America's books about boys."[33]

Partly Tom Sawyer and partly Penrod, but mostly a self-portrait of

Cobb as a thirteen-year-old boy in Paducah, Juney Custer has all the social reticences of his literary counterparts. Badgering his school teacher to punish him by substituting for his velvet costume a girls' sunbonnet and apron, he meets the challenge of the Fauntleroy suit with an ingenuity that can command the respect of any other boy-hero in American literature. All in all, with an adolescent flair of his own he leads his small corps of companions in the traditional treasure-hunting, the promoting of neighborhood side-shows, and the setting up of lemonade stands (though Juney specializes in fresh fruit and "lickrish water"). He also forms societies and organizations like the "Going Round Doing Good Club," which is an adolescent fusion of the Salvation Army and the Pickwick Club. But his humane enterprises are doomed to achieve nothing save the most inhumane results. In the classic style of boys' neighborhood clubs everywhere, this one arranges a single combat between Juney and a small, wiry bully named Banty Gearin, who later dies heroically while saving another boy from drowning.

Few episodes in any of the so-called "boys' books" can surpass in sheer vigor and broad comedy Cobb's narrative of the wholesale havoc wrought by a cat whose head is caught in an empty salmon can. If there is a more entertaining boyhood episode anywhere in Cobb's fiction, it is the bizarre story of the "canning" of a dog that escapes from his tormentors and, with a teakettle clattering behind, dashes through a sedate funeral cortege, upsetting the hearse. The coffin then tumbles down a slope, falls open, and comes to rest on its foot end, with its occupant, a deceased local veterinarian, directly facing the frightened culprits, who are hiding under a bridge. "I know that the greatest thrill I ever had," says Cobb in the last sentence of this story, "was when for the first, last, and only time in my life I met Old Doc Wheeler face to face."[34] Whenever Cobb engages in boyhood reminiscences, he is likely to refer to this episode.

In one important way, however, the reminiscing and fictionalizing that have come out of Irvin Cobb's boyhood in Paducah are different from the writings of most other childhood authors. The distinguishing feature of Cobb's writing—both fact and fiction—is that much of the best has come from his childhood fascination with and his true reverence for the older people in the community, especially for those who were aged but still vigorous and full of reminiscence. As a boy, Cobb had one trait of character that seems most rare in the young of any time—the capacity to understand and to cherish a truth which has been best phrased by Old Judge Priest, that for an old man "the past is about all he's got to look forward to."[35]

Later, as a prolific writer of fiction, Cobb seemed able to recall every detail of yarning sessions with older men and of the yarns themselves. Moreover, with often no more than a transparent alteration of a name, he drew from these real people the characters of his fiction: Old Judge Priest, Jeff Poindexter, Sergeant Jimmy Bagby, Dr. Lake, and most of the other characters who regularly inhabit the fiction that might be called his "Back Home" stories. "It was worth any boy's while," wrote Cobb, "to listen to the company that assembled on Judge Priest's front porch."[36]

The *Daily News:* Eager Cub and Boy Editor

Like most Paducah boys who were growing up during the 1880s and 1890s, Irvin Cobb tried his hand at a variety of odd jobs and piece work during his years in school. He delivered circulars and carried newspapers. By the time he was fifteen, he knew that he had a potentially valuable talent for drawing cartoons and caricatures. He had developed that talent sufficiently to sell four pictures to a weekly magazine, though he apparently never received any pay. For a time he considered pursuing a career as artist or illustrator, and during his early newspaper days he sometimes illustrated his own stories. But his interest in writing gradually superseded his ambition to wield a drawing pencil. For a considerable time he drove an ice wagon in the summertime, and this experience furnished him a large number of anecdotes for future use. He forsook all these interests and occupations along with his formal education when he realized that his family depended upon him for financial support.

Within his first few days as a cub reporter for the old *Paducah Daily News,* Irvin Cobb became a confirmed and dedicated newspaperman. For the rest of his life, no matter how lofty his success as a writer of fiction, he preferred to think of himself as a journalist. During his later years as a "veteran reporter," he became fond of observing that in all the newspaper shops he had ever known—whether large paper or small, whether metropolitan or small-town—the characteristic odors of the newspaper office invariably induced in him a feeling of challenge and excitement. Toward the end of his career he observed that this "alluring stench" had always been with him, "binding me fast to the workbench of the journeyman scrivener. One way or another it has shaped my course for all my days. I have no regrets. It has taken me where the wheels of the world went 'round" (*EL,* 93).

To a young man who had sacrificed all chance to study law in favor of a job that was supposed to bring money into a household, Irvin Cobb's first weeks as a reporter were barren of encouragement. To any boy less enamoured of the work for its own sake, these first weeks on the *Daily News* might have spelled the death rather than the birth of a career, since during that time Irvin received no pay and was given no promise that he could expect any.

For a while before taking the job, he had toyed with the idea of going to work as a call boy for one of the railroads, starting at three dollars a week. But when his father inquired whether he would prefer a job with the newspaper for which Joel Shrewsbury had written so many provocative articles, Irvin remembered those times when he had kept the old man company during their composition. He remembered also the times when "Uncle" Jo had said to him, as though imparting something personal and predictive, "you couldn't start too soon training a boy for a journalistic career" (*M,* 22). Moreover, though Cobb had never had the "head for figures" which was essential to commercial careers, he had always been far ahead of his schoolmates in reading, speaking, argument, and composition, all of which promised much for one who sought a career in journalism. So he had walked into the newspaper office at the appointed time and had become an unpaid cub reporter.

He does not seem to have been much concerned about the question of pay. In several places he has recounted the story of his experiences on the old *Daily News* as well as the story of his early newspaper training in general, and in looking back upon the beginning of his career he conveys the impression that, despite his urgent need for money, he was more concerned with proving his worth as a reporter than with being paid. He was only sixteen years old, and being perfectly familiar with the small-town way of doing such things, he took the job in the faith that he would be paid something whenever he had made himself valuable enough to be placed on the payroll. This moment of truth occurred on the Saturday night of his third week, when his boss gave him a handful of coins amounting to one dollar and seventy-five cents. Within four months of this event he was earning four dollars a week, which in 1893 was a dramatic increase for a man so young and for one with so short a time on the job.

Cobb could hardly have found a newspaper office better equipped to provide the basic training for a future "star reporter," for a popular humorist, and for a leading writer of fiction. In the early 1890s the *Paducah Daily News* was a small evening daily with a weekly edition that consisted mostly of material reprinted from the issues of the previous week. Fundamentally it was a good shop, operated by men who had served hard apprenticeships in the printing trades, who knew from practical experience the special demands of small-town newspaper work, and whose professional values were sound if severely provincial.

Because the town was a transportation hub for a large and busy region, the local newspaper—which in Cobb's time might otherwise have been only a weekly in a town of similar size—the readership of the *Daily News* was larger and somewhat more cosmopolitan than other small-town papers. Therefore the professional standards of the *Daily News* staff were higher than one might expect, even though the whole operation was geared to serving a small community and was by modern standards perceptibly unsophisticated. The commercial flavor of the town appealed to those journalistic vagabonds known as "drifters" or "tramp printers." Many of these were journalists of high talent and of impressive but tarnished literary reputation, and they went from one newspaper job to another, quitting when they became bored, or merely disappearing without explanation. Of these the *Daily News* always had more than its share, and from them a reportorial cub like Irvin Cobb was able to learn much about the craft of writing.

The shop was dominated by the character and personality of one "Boss Jim," who managed the business side of the enterprise, and who employed his brother as editor, along with a scattering of near and distant relatives in other positions. For this reason, and because there appears to have been little favoritism on family grounds, those who were not related to the boss felt literally that they were accepted members of a professional "family."

The relationships between the newspaper and the community were very close. Residents of the town had a strong proprietary interest in whatever happened at the shop, not only because their news organ was by slant avowedly Democratic in an almost rabidly Democratic section, but also because "Boss Jim" held a kind of open house for townsfolk who enjoyed stopping by to read the news exchanges, to talk with the staff, or merely to pass the time of day.

Anybody in the place was welcome to participate in a ritual that could have arisen and been perpetuated only in a small-town newspaper. Indeed, this particular ritual must have been unique to the *Daily*

News. Whenever a subscriber came to renew his two-dollar subscription, "Boss Jim" dropped one dollar into the cashier's box, and with the other he led a procession from the newspaper office into a nearby saloon, where he bought everybody in his following a glass of whiskey at ten cents a shot. Besides being a most agreeable ceremony for the newspaper employees, this custom was an effective device for public relations.

At first, Cobb was the only member of the staff who was supposed to devote his time exclusively to the gathering of local news, though the paper was top-heavy with special editors who served also in the capacity of reporter from time to time. Cobb soon developed an appreciation for "news values," and he could be counted upon to furnish the managing editor with enough "personals" to fill one or two columns of print each day. Having discovered one of the basic axioms of newspapering—that people like to see their names in print—he became a ubiquitous figure wherever busses stopped, boats docked, goods were offered for public sale, or people gathered in hotel lobbies. As young as he was, he perceived that everything people did was interesting to other people, and like any good newsman he possessed the curiosity which drove him to investigate.

Thirty years after Cobb's death, one of his Paducah friends remarked, "The big difference between Irvin Cobb and most of the rest of us is that he found out exactly what he could do in this life, and he never wasted his time trying to do anything else."[37] Convinced that he was in the right business for his talents, he did everything possible to develop those talents. But since it seemed to Cobb that the development of talent meant making the most of one's individual strengths, he unleashed himself in ways that might have been, and sometimes were, troublesome for his employers.

At first he illustrated his stories with his own chalk drawings, and when his zest for news gathering replaced his interest in illustration, he began prying into hitherto unexploited areas of business and social activity in order to unearth fresh sources for news. He haunted the railroad shops to pick up whatever might have been the turn-of-century variety of "scuttlebutt," and he pestered the river editor to let him roam the waterfronts in search of the adventurous tales which the old river pilots were forever spinning.

He learned to make news stories out of gossip and romantic yarning, and he was sometimes piqued when the editor cut them out of the paper in favor of the same old "personals" which Cobb regularly supplied. Later, Cobb was to realize that the editor's sense of news values was the right one for a small-town paper. Yet nothing could ever blunt the edge of Cobb's fascination with the "human interest" aspect of news gathering. As a big city "star reporter" he was to capitalize over and over again upon the human side of the news, while other veteran newsmen were trying futilely to scrape up regular news stories from the standard sources.

Of all the advantages which the *Daily News* could offer a young reporter, none was so valuable as the opportunity to learn all phases of the publishing process. Cobb learned the busy job printing operation, the advertising, and the general business side, as well as every angle of reportorial work. Together, these led him straight into top editorial positions. As a reporter, he was eventually entrusted with such delicate assignments as the covering of city council meetings, but along the way he had covered almost everything else that could fall to a cub reporter: "court proceedings, trials, crimes, accidents, deaths, notices of shows that came to the opera house, business changes—even paragraphs of a supposedly humorous nature. I covered the county fair . . . weddings and political rallies, revival meetings and the openings of new saloons" (*M,* 35).

All in all, he found himself writing at least four or five complete columns of material a day, even though the haste of such composition exaggerated his weakness in spelling. The editor corrected the most glaring of such errors but was apparently so grateful for a man who could turn out large amounts of interesting copy that he overlooked the technical alterations. This form of editorial encouragement had a peculiar effect upon Cobb's development as a writer. He was aware that "the freedom of it bred in me the joy of creation and encouraged me constantly to keep enlarging the scope of my writings; but the absence of any editorial discipline made me careless of results and freakish and fresh" (*M,* 37).

By the time he was nineteen, Cobb had become managing editor of the *Daily News.* Thereupon, other newspaper men in Kentucky and the surrounding region began referring to him as the "boy editor."[38] By a rapid succession of advances, each the result of the death or retirement of old hands on the staff, Cobb had gone from cub to full-fledged reporter and on to managing editor within his first three years of work as a professional journalist.

During his few months in this position, the paper printed under Cobb's picture a secondary caption that identified him as "The youngest managing editor of a daily paper in the United States."[39] However remarkable Cobb's dramatic rise may have seemed to others, Cobb looked back upon the phenomenon skeptically and with the objectivity that made him a successful humorist.

Whether he had been the youngest editor he did not know for sure, but as he viewed this episode from the vantage of real maturity, he declared, "I'm sure I was the worst managing editor of any age in the United States. I was reckless, smart-alecky, careless, gaudy in my enthusiasms, a dynamic builder of lurid headlines. I rarely let a dull fact hamper my style" (*EL,* 96). Considering these unsettling characteristics, along with the large number of law suits that accrued to his garish headlining, Cobb has never been surprised that after several months, in sheer self-protection, the owners of the paper put a mature newsman in the editorship and sent Irvin back to the reportorial ranks.

Local Correspondent: Lure of the Big-Time

Irvin Cobb did not feel the lure of the city newspapers until, at the age of twenty, he had become the local correspondent for so many metropolitan papers that he could see the disadvantages in his remaining forever a small-town newsman. One vantage in his seeking work on a metropolitan paper was that its reporters had to be better writers than most small-town reporters were, and that the metropolitan newsman was therefore rarely asked to provide so large a bulk of written material for each issue. After a few years on the Paducah paper, Cobb had found himself yearning to write well instead of voluminously, and to measure his journalistic talents against those of the best men in the profession. Moreover, he could not deny the increasing attractiveness of higher pay scales. When he began to realize that his weekly correspondent's pay frequently equaled or surpassed his regular salary from the *Daily News,* he began to feel that his destiny as a journalist could be fulfilled only in a metropolitan area.

Any doubts disappeared when Joseph Medill of the *Chicago Tribune* sent him a hundred dollars for covering a single news story that had broken in a town near Paducah. To Cobb, so large a check seemed a windfall. "Here in one magnificent packet," he writes, "was as much as I made in salary in two months. It was the largest amount I had ever owned at one time in my life. It was hard to believe. If a man working one night could make that much off of a city paper how much could he make in a month or a year? . . . From that hour dated my desire to work on a big newspaper, by preference a Chicago or New York newspaper. I wanted to get there before mad extravagance plunged them into bankruptcy" (*EL,* 110–11).

The circumstances under which Cobb wrote this first lucrative story have been fully described in both *Myself—To Date* and *Exit Laughing.* The episode is particularly important in Cobb's career because it is the first journalistic assignment in which Cobb demonstrated his ingenuity and his capacity for decisive action. For several months the Chicago police had chased a murderer and his accomplice all over the country and had thereby created a great deal of lurid national publicity. Then some local police captured the culprits and jailed them in a small Kentucky town about a hundred miles from Paducah. Instantly responding to a blanket call from the Chicago Tribune to all the local correspondents in that part of the country, Cobb found himself the only *Tribune* correspondent on the scene, competing for the story against veteran staff men from most of the other big-city papers.

While a deputy with a rifle kept these seasoned reporters away from the prisoners, Cobb went directly to the mayor of the town, who had served with "Josh" Cobb in the Confederate army. From this official he obtained consent to visit the prisoners in their cell. Cobb not only "scooped" all the veteran reporters in getting the interview, but he also beat them in transmitting his story to his Chicago paper. While several other newsmen monopolized the Western Union wires and exhausted the operator with background material before they could file their complete stories, Cobb went to the railroad postal operator, and by writing furiously for several hours, sent to the *Tribune* the only complete and accurate account of the flight and capture of the two criminals, who had become notorious all over the country as "Merry and Smith." Many times in later years, when Cobb was himself a veteran reporter for the big newspapers, he managed to accomplish similar coups.

The Mastering of the Trade

In his five or six years as reporter and as "boy editor" for the *Daily News,* Cobb had laid the foundation for every successful job as reporter, editor, public speaker, humorist, playwright, familiar essayist, and fiction writer that was to come his way in a career as varied and as prolific as that of any American writer of his generation. If he had not yet acquired the self-assurance and the deceptive, back-yonder sophistication that later became signal qualities of his character, he had found out who he was and what he could do best.

As a writer he had overcome most of the cuteness and gaucheries that almost every young journalist mistakes for "style." Further, in being stripped of romantic illusions about newspapering, he had acquired sound professional values and was able to establish realistic goals for himself. He had discovered that "reporting, like any other specialized work, is a trade to be learned, not one to be born with. And I learned mine. I acquired it by experience, by making the same mistake so often that, after a while, I learned not to make it quite so often."[40]

In ways that were sometimes painful, he had learned the limits of brashness and eccentricity in good prose style, and by direct experience he had become sensitive to the need for taste in whatever he wrote for a broad reading public. Above all, he was now safely beyond those amateurish stages of composition that every good writer must pass on his way to maturity as a craftsman. As Cobb describes this phase of his development, "I was beginning to get cured of the adolescent belief that the only good writing was this so-called fine writing, full of adjectives and screaming metaphors and reverberating periods. In other words, I had quit writing at the top of my voice" (M, 84).

All these things he had learned as adolescent boy and as young man in his home town of Paducah, and to Paducah he gave the credit throughout his life. In looking back upon the beginning of his career, in remembering the hard first steps by which he had started on his way, he sometimes berated those young authors who always seem to feel that there is an easy way to learn one of the hardest and most precarious of crafts. "It is the green, raw, untried hand who is so gosh-awful confident, not the seasoned performer," he warns. "It is the untried fledgling who puts so high a value upon himself, not the old-timer, who knows by bitter experience how very easy it is to fail, even though he has worked very hard to avoid failure."

As a writer of fiction, moreover, in looking back upon his childhood in Paducah, he realized how much he owed to that time and that place. Speaking of his fictional characters, he once remarked, "There is always the mysterious moulding process in the mind from which a type in fiction springs in after life. He blooms in the seed planted unconsciously in the past, the never-to-be-forgotten past. I suppose our boyhood belongs to that period."[42] Wherever he went, an important part of Irvin Cobb remained in Paducah, just as Paducah lived in Cobb's fiction.

Chapter Two
Newspaper Minion

Whatever may have been the heights of Irvin Cobb's ambition as a freshly weaned newspaper cub in Paducah, the idea of seeking a position on the staff of a big Eastern daily did not yet occur to him. As he sought ways of moving into higher professional and economic brackets, he thought first of those comparatively large urban papers that had employed him as their local correspondent in Paducah. For these papers, as for Joseph Medill's *Chicago Tribune,* he had already demonstrated his competence as a newsman, and it seemed to him a relatively easy step to move from local correspondent to resident staff member on one or another of these large and sophisticated newspapers.

As Cobb was to find in his climb to the top of a profession which he had entered as an adolescent—and which through a long and active life he never really left—none of the steps up the ladder was as easy as it seemed. In making his first moves at an age when other boys were still in college, Cobb began to establish a pattern that prevailed throughout his career. In every newspaper position he ever held, except for the two years immediately after his marriage, he mastered the requirements of the job speedily and was ready to move to a higher one as soon as he knew he could qualify. He preferred to accept the risks of early advancement over the stagnation of "coasting."

First Big Job: A Bad Shop

During Cobb's first few days with a metropolitan newspaper, his dreams of success turned to nightmare. So unsavory and so disillusioning was this first trial that whenever he refers to it Cobb has been seized with uncharacteristic delicacy. In *Myself—to Date* (1923), apparently wishing to speak his mind without identifying the newspaper by name, he mentions only "a paper printed in a city of a quarter million or so, in a state to the north of us" (*M,* 84). In *Exit Laughing* (1941), he apparently thought it the better part of discretion to avoid mentioning the incident altogether.

This paper was the *Cincinnati Post.* At that time it was not an independent newspaper, but only one in a considerable chain of afternoon dailies whose editorial and personnel policies were determined in some remote administrative office. "The *Post* was run on weird lines," remarks Cobb in what he seems to have considered gross understatement, and at the end of the paragraph he says, "the whole establishment spent most of its time standing on its head and whirling around" (*M,* 85).

In spite of his diverse experiences on the Paducah paper, he was aware that in any metropolitan shop he was the greenest kind of raw recruit, though as he confessed later, "I was full of pleasing delusions about myself" (*M,* 84). Going to work in the telegraph room, he was appalled by the dust, noise, and universal confusion. No editor could remain long enough in his job to establish a policy before he was demoted or fired. Then he relinquished the job to some other man who did his best to establish his own system for handling the news before he, too, was removed by the unpredictable fiat of a top boss who made all command decisions from a distant office. Much later in his career, Cobb was fond of debunking the widespread myth that "a newspaper shop is run like a madhouse and that as the hour of going to press approaches it becomes more of a madhouse than ever, being peopled with agitated figures rushing wildly to and fro and uttering demoniac shrieks."[1] He had apparently forgotten that he once worked for a large paper where every hour of every day was nearly such a madhouse.

He doggedly remained on this distasteful job for a month before he fell victim to one of the wholesale purges and reshufflings of personnel. Without "any degree of finesse" (*M,* 88), his boss told Cobb that he was no longer employed there, and Cobb returned jobless to Paducah. He was angry and chastened, but relieved. Though he would not go back to the *Cincinnati Post* under any conditions (the paper tried to hire him again in only a few days), he was already excited by the prospects of landing a job with another big regional newspaper whose professional standards might match his expectations, and where his talent could flourish under a higher challenge.

Funny Stuff: "Sourmash"

When Irvin Cobb went to work for the *Louisville Evening Post* at a salary of eighteen dollars a week in the fall of 1898, he was twenty-three years old. But by now he was not quite the "sap-green" small-town newsman who had reported for work on the Cincinnati paper six weeks earlier. Though in years he was not measurably older, he was now vastly more mature in his perspective. If he had lost many of his illusions about the journalist's life, the illusions that he had lost were for the most part expendable illusions.

In less than a year on the Louisville paper, Cobb had established himself as a willing and reliable newsman. He appears to have had a good working relationship with his superiors, and after the first few months his editors began to relieve him of routine assignments in order to take advantage of his ingenuity in digging out and developing feature stories and other so-called "human interest" material. One of the first continuing features he introduced was a humorous column that appeared irregularly at first, but always under the boxed heading "Sourmash." The head was printed in large longhand script, with an elaborately wrought capital *S* at the beginning and a rough longhand period at the end.[2] The column began appearing in 1900 and was being published regularly by 1901, except when Cobb was away on assignment as staff correspondent in another city, where he could not follow the highly topical events of local interest that made up a considerable part of the "Sourmash" column.

Cobb's choice of title for this column is a brilliant stroke of professional acumen for so young a journalist. To all Kentucky newspaper readers, but especially to those readers from the great central bluegrass and from the eastern Kentucky mountains, the word "sourmash" was full of subtle, highly personal implications, and it was fraught with cultural significance. As far back as the earliest pioneer times in the "Old Southwest," Kentucky had fostered the growth of a unique and a deeply respected social class, the "bourbon aristocracy." For generation after generation these landholders had passed on to their sons the precious "distils," or merely "stills" as they came to be known in popular idiom, and the distilleries were far more important to these families than the land or the livestock.

Of all the social classes in Kentucky, none has been more highly respected than the "bourbon aristocracy." Families of this special class have been considered genteel, and even those families that fell upon hard times in the prohibition era lost little of their gentility. Eventually Irvin Cobb was to write the only American novel based upon and celebrating the "bourbon aristocracy."[3] As early as 1901 he was aware that nothing else could evoke such pride or create such unstudied enthusiasm among his readers as could the single word "Sourmash" at the head of his column.

"Sourmash" was Cobb's first sustained attempt at humorous writing on the comparatively sophisticated level of metropolitan journalism. He remarks that he had once "turned out bales of bum jingles and supposedly humorous comment on local subjects. And he [the Paducah editor] was good enough to compliment it."[4] For the few months of its existence[5] this column was one of the most frequently quoted of all the regular features in the *Evening Post*.

Sometimes the column was in appallingly bad taste, and much of the humor was painfully obvious, but Kentucky readers enjoyed Cobb's unaffected "down yonder" tone and his wry observations upon the fallibility of human nature. Cobb had not yet passed beyond his indulgence in the writing of what he later called "alleged verses,"[6] and from time to time his "Sourmash" readers were treated to a piece of versifying in this vein: "They tell it o'er the countryside / At eventide and morn / That the fodder all was shocked / At the stripping of the corn" (11 June 1901).

At least 95 percent of "Sourmash" is devoted to the mildly amusing if sometimes inept humor that has always characterized the topical content of most humorous newspaper columns. The content of "Sourmash" has a strongly political slant, and most of the material makes fun of well-known political figures who are in the news at the time. Yet all of Cobb's items are not intended as comic. In the column for 30 May 1901, for instance, this "booster" appears: "Our worthy mayor should go to Congress and become chairman of the Committee on Foreign Relations. All his home relations have been looked after in a most satisfactory manner."

Nationally prominent political figures, those who were widely quoted and whose names and faces were familiar to almost everybody in America, sometimes became targets of relentless joshing in Cobb's "Sourmash." William Jennings Bryan, for example, became almost as much a subject for verbal caricature in "Sourmash" as he was a perennial subject for the political cartoonists of the time.

For the "Sourmash" column, Cobb created the first in a long succession of his wise, independent, eccentric, homespun, and deceptively simple "back-porch philosophers," of whom the incomparable Judge Priest would eventually be the most viable and the most fully developed example. A humorous column of one kind or another was a prominent feature of most large newspapers at this time, and it was a common device of these journalistic humorists to dramatize and add variety to their columns by creating an imaginary character whom they could "quote" as delivering some of the cleverist quips in the column.

In humorous columns all over the nation, these imaginary quipsters ran the gamut from the clever and the sophisticated to the clown and the simpleton.

In "Sourmash" Cobb introduced to his readers the character of "Uncle Dudley Pennyrile." Sometimes referring to him as "Uncle Dud," Cobb endowed him with the kind of Southern speech that would be typical of such a character, even though Cobb carefully wrote the rest of the column in standard journalistic style and diction. The basic character of "Uncle Dud" emerges clearly from the kinds of things he chooses to say, from the uncommon sense of his assertions, and from the unaffectedly colloquial mode in which he expresses himself. Through the character of "Uncle Dud," Cobb could add color to matters of local color, as in this "Sourmash" entry (12 June 1901): "Uncle Dudley Pennyrile says he knows towns in Kentucky where the enumerator could git the results the easiest way by just dropping down to the depot at train time. Uncle Dud says he would find everybody there except them that was in bed or jail." In the same column, Cobb offers this cracker-barrel perversion of an old saw: "Uncle Dudley Pennyrile says its a long lane that has no saloon."

In "Sourmash," for the first time in his career, Irvin Cobb began to exploit his extraordinary capacity for discovering popular humor in the limitless nuances of American speech. The most casual reading of any typical "Sourmash" column reveals Cobb's readiness to twist the language into a complicated pun, or to weave complex and sometimes farfetched puns into other kinds of humorous material. Besides the youthful exuberance of his punning, however, the sheer incongruity of familiar place names frequently provided him with a local-colorist brand of humor that appealed strongly to the tastes of his Kentucky readers. Sometimes his readers must have wished that they, instead of Cobb, might have been the first to say, "One of the troubles of Kentucky is that Murder Creek does not run into Hanging Fork" (5 June 1901).

To Cobb, this early experience as a humorist was priceless. Here he learned that the foundations of effective humor are the same at all levels of society, needing only to be adapted to different circumstances through alterations in levels of taste and through devices of language. Cobb's inexhaustible variations upon all kinds of topical humor eventually accounted for the universal success of his many humorous books and his dozens of humorous articles in America's best "slick" magazines.

The Statehouse: Politics and Murder

For long periods Cobb had to suspend the daily publication of "Sour-mash" in order to report political activities in other sections of the state. He frequently stayed for weeks or months in the Kentucky cap-ital of Frankfort, which was the center of high-level politics in the state. Even before the time when "Sourmash" had established itself as one of the most widely read features in the *Louisville Post,* Cobb had begun working as a regular political reporter and had established a temporary residence in Frankfort. Here, working as the "capital cor-respondent" or the "statehouse reporter,"[7] he found himself not merely covering one of Kentucky's most sensational murder trials but inad-vertently playing a personal role in events connected with the murder.

More precisely, this affair generated a great deal of Machiavellian political intrigue which culminated in a sordid and lurid political as-sassination. In this nearly incredible but true-life drama of power pol-itics, murder by ambush, and supercharged pyrotechnics in the courtroom, the central figure was a grotesque and demagogue named William Goebel. A sinister figure who in repose reminded Cobb of "a snake about to strike" (*EL,* 201),[8] Goebel had seized Kentucky by its unprotected throat in the aftermath of the first Republican victory in the history of the commonwealth. Before this "political forebear of Huey Long" (*EL,* 200) had taken the oath of office, someone shot him mortally from the window of an office building in the Statehouse Square in Frankfort.

All through the ensuing campaign Cobb had watched incredulously and with grudging admiration as this calculating egomaniac increased his own advantages by perpetrating one outrage after another upon his opponents, his constituents, and the innocent people of Kentucky. At the moment of assassination, Cobb was in a position to tell the whole story from the beginning of the campaign, through the crowded and intricate maneuverings of the individual trials, and on to the convic-tion of those conspirators who were judged responsible for the death of the new governor. The trial was a rallying point for explosive political factions that kept Kentucky "on the raw edge of civil war."[9]

In Irvin Cobb's apprenticeship as an author, this series of trials was an important event. At the time of the murder, by a singular turn of circumstance, Cobb was rolling up his sleeves in a washroom on the first floor of the legislature. He heard the fatal shots and ran out a side door in his shirtsleeves in time to help three men carry the dying Goebel from the capital grounds to a nearby hotel. As soon as possible, Cobb took detailed statements from all three of these men, and he was the first reporter in the whole corps of capital correspondents to piece together a coherent account of the event and to get it onto the wires to his paper in Louisville.[10]

Cobb sat through the ensuing trials, taking exhaustive notes on the proceedings in a form of shorthand that he had devised for his own use. For the rest of his life, Cobb made the best use of this ingenious tool of his profession. By employing this device he was able to record almost verbatim long passages of direct discourse and formal testimony. By the time he had piled up more than 600,000 words of accurate testimony during the first murder trial of Harry Thaw in 1907, his editors on the *New York World* insisted that he was capable of producing more printable copy each day than three or four other reporters combined.[11]

Like the young Charles Dickens, who had devised a similar system for recording testimony and procedures in the English courts, Cobb achieved so sensitive a coordination of eye and ear that all the nuances of speech and gesture were indelibly impressed upon his memory, ready for the day when he first tried his hand at the writing of fiction. Hardly any other form of training could have been more useful to a fictioneer who specialized in re-creating through phrasing and orthography the graphic and picturesque oral dialects of Southerners, of New Yorkers, and even Far Westerners.

Back Home: Editor and Family Man

During the Goebel trial, Irvin Cobb had married. The courtship had been long and unlikely, and on the surface the marital union between Irvin Cobb and Laura Spencer Baker of Savannah seems to have been even more unlikely. In almost everything they were opposites, except in that profound respect that outweighed all the others—their utter and unreserved devotion to each other.

To their daughter "Buff" in after years, it seemed incredible that two people from such widely different family backgrounds and social circumstances could ever have formed more than a passing acquaintance with each other. Irvin was very tall, so skinny that he was sometimes called "Shrivly," and full of roughshod independence that marks the native of a frontier river town, while Laura was "little and dark and pretty and merry and literal-minded and conservative and easily shocked—enthusiastic, very impatient, quicksilver to move, passionately loyal, and about as non-literary as a literate person can be."[12] Today, old timers in Paducah remember the home of the Thornbury girls, who were close friends and classmates of Laura Baker at Nashville's Belmont College. These local girls frequently brought Laura home to visit with them during vacations,[13] and through their wide circle of friends in Paducah, Laura first met Irvin Cobb.

At the time of their marriage in her home in Savannah on 12 June 1900, Laura had impulsively unbetrothed herself from another young man, and Irvin had taken short leave from his job with the *Louisville Post*. For the next few years, he gave salary and security first priorities over all other considerations, and when the new owner of the daily paper in Paducah offered him four dollars a week more than his Louisville salary, he left Louisville straightaway, went home to Paducah, and set up housekeeping with his bride of ten months. After a series of escalating offers from Louisville, whose editors wanted him back at any price within the boundaries of their salary scale, Cobb had accepted Colonel Woodson's last counteroffer of thirty dollars a month. Upon this conspicuously inflated salary, especially since the Louisville paper had reluctantly declined to make a higher bid, Cobb felt that he could afford to settle down in Paducah as a managing editor. He was in a far different shop and a far different job from the one upon which he had foundered as the precocious teenage editor of the *Paducah Daily News* in 1893. The old business had been bought and sold several times since Cobb had gone to Cincinnati. Now, under the ownership and management of a respected upstate publisher, the whole plant had been fitted out with the newest machinery, and these sophisticated improvements gave the *Daily Democrat* and its immediate successor, the *News Democrat,* a highly competitive potential for papers of this kind and class.

To an editor as conscientious and painstaking as Cobb, the responsibilities of the new position were all-consuming. Usually understaffed and without competent help in the editorial routine, Cobb personally wrote substantial amounts of daily copy. Moreover, he found that he had to edit every item prepared by the reportorial staff, the feature writers, and the special correspondents. Partly from habit and partly from his conviction that the quality and the reputation of the journal required his personal supervision of all final copy, he corrected as many of the daily proof sheets as he could before the copy went into the back shop for composing and printing. He worked out all headings and prepared all the exchanges. Because the new paper was officially a member of the Associated Press, Cobb also chose appropriate syndicated articles and edited them for local use.

Somehow Cobb always met the deadlines for six regular editions during the week, but the special Sunday issue became more and more a drain upon his energies. He refused to allow in this issue any other copy than purely local material, and he insisted that it be fresh and lively. Because for the special issue he denied himself the quick and easy borrowing of articles from outside sources and from other places, the Sunday edition began to seem to him "a hungry, yawning thing" (*M,* 99). Despite the increasing toll upon his nervous system, his emotional stability, and his general health, he remained the managing editor of the *Paducah News-Democrat* for two and a half years. Because he had developed an extraordinary capacity for managing many different operations at once, and because he insisted upon maintaining the highest possible standards in every operation, the paper flourished.

At this moment in his career, Cobb was trapped in the bread-winner syndrome, as are most of the typical middle-class Americans who must put their families before everything else, and who spend respectable, productive, but uninspired lives until they must account to death or retirement. Hemingway later observed of the effects of newswriting upon his own fiction, "Newspaper work is valuable up until the point that it forcibly begins to destroy your memory. A writer must leave it before that point."[14] Indeed, as each day Cobb had to purge his mind of yesterday's dead or dying news, he was blunting the edge of the accurate and comprehensive memory upon which, as a prolific writer of fiction, he later drew incessantly.

Yet, even in this stifling routine, Cobb managed to learn something of surpassing value about the creative process. Other editors might have taken the easy way to fill space in the daily editions—by loading the columns with bare-fact reports that came over the syndicate wire—but Cobb selected only those skeleton communications that had some local appeal. By the most subtle exercise of his intuition and his imagination, he fleshed out the bare-bones accounts with descriptive and narrative details which so closely fitted those actual events that even witnesses were convinced that Cobb or one of his reporters must have had firsthand knowledge. Among veteran newspaper men, this practice was called "smoking up a story," and few men could equal Cobb in the completeness and the credibility of a finished account. He could "smoke up" a vivid and believable story equally well for a local event or for a wired dispatch.[15]

In no other profession, and particularly in no other situation than his present one, would Cobb have been so challenged to exercise his imagination in order to achieve the verisimilitude of preexisting facts. Each time he did so, he sharpened and broadened his capacity to blend fiction and reality. Eventually he would discover that he could write fiction in much the same way. When the combination worked as it should, the result was a well-paced, carefully balanced, vigorously narrated product of the imagination. It had the simplicity, the directness, and the credibility of a good human-interest story by any top-notch journalist.

But otherwise, after two years of slow disintegration in mind and body under the pressures of an intolerable work load, Cobb began to think again of the opulent big-city newspapers. There, a good reporter might earn a top salary for doing a specialized job better than any other man. Until now, he realized, he had been unaware that his diminutive wife was a creature of surprising courage and self-sufficiency. Moreover, she had such faith in Cobb as to make him wonder whether he could justify her trust. Even though he had to ask Laura and the baby to live with her parents for a time, and even though he had to borrow two hundred dollars from his father-in-law to make the trip, she insisted that he go to New York. He was to do everything in his power to get himself established in the newspaper job he wanted. Then he could send for his wife and daughter.

He had made the break almost too late. Because there had been no place for a sense of humor among the higher priorities of his work as editor, that precious sense had languished. Moreover, the responsibilities of marriage had made him serious-minded, and for three years after he first went to work for the *Daily Democrat* he had made no attempt at humorous writing. For a time, it seems, Irvin Cobb had lost his sense of humor.

How to Insult the Editors and Get a Job

Among Irvin Cobb's critics and biographers there is a tendency to write flippantly about the episode in which the country boy from Paducah tames New York City. Cobb's good friend Robert H. Davis, for instance, tells of Irvin's going to the big town "buoyed up by the illusion that he was needed there along with other reforms."[16] Cobb's daughter "Buff," whose own sense of humor is far too sprightly ever to be suppressed, vividly recounts the events which led to her father's getting "the only genuine simon-pure inspiration he ever did have, and he knew that it came from on high because it worked."[17]

But before Cobb had whatever shrewd idea he called an "inspiration," he spent two weeks of almost unbearable loneliness, discouragement, and outright rejection by the city which thousands of aspiring young people left in suicidal despair every year. Here he was, trying to "crash" New York City journalism at the time of year when every newspaper in town was laying off every possible man. These yearly cuts and layoffs frequently included experienced reporters whose only hope was to return when hiring began a few months later, when they would be rehired before all other applicants—ahead of unknown job-hunters like Irvin Cobb.

From his cramped hall bedroom on the fourth floor of a rooming house on West Fifty-Seventh Street, Cobb had launched a determined campaign to penetrate beyond the outer office of every major newspaper in New York. He sent to the editors copies of impressive letters of recommendation that he had carried from Paducah, and he made daily rounds of personal visitation, going to the evening papers during morning hours and to the morning papers in the afternoon. But for two weeks he failed to get past a single office boy. Even the personal efforts of so influential a man as his old publisher Colonel Woodson proved to be useless. The answer was the same everywhere: there were no openings.

Short of some miraculous windfall, Cobb knew at the end of those two weeks that his miscalculation of the real costs of city living would soon leave him destitute. Yet almost every afternoon he felt justified in making an extra draft upon his lean purse—for public transportation into some remote neighborhood of the great city, where he wandered until darkness or hunger drove him back to his barren rooms on Fifty-Seventh Street. Like Charles Dickens, who never grew tired of wandering the streets of London at night, Irvin Cobb had a compulsion to see unfamiliar places and to observe all sorts of people. Among his earliest and best-known short stories are several whose sources lie directly in things he saw or heard while he wandered alone in these far-flung and sometimes forbidding corners of the city.

But he was also making a close analysis of all the metropolitan newspapers, and he found that the blasé, worldly, and basically irreverent "sophistication" of the New Yorkers was matched by a correspondingly flippant, cavalier, and lightly cynical style of journalism that prevailed in the New York journals. To Irvin Cobb, this tone seemed to be much like the deliberately sly and humorous tone of many items that he had written for the "Sourmash" column. "Where I'd come from," he writes, "you didn't get humorous in print at the expense of persons of standing in the community, unless you craved excitement and felt the need of a little violent personal exercise. Here in this town nobody seemed too high and mighty to be jibed by reporters and headliners" (M, 116).

This discovery led him to the "simon-pure inspiration" that told him what course he must take. At first the idea seemed a desperate one. But his understanding of the vagaries of his profession, his firsthand knowledge of the editorial mind, and his thorough analysis of his own peculiar situation told him that his idea was as safe as any informed risk could ever be. So he composed a short form letter, using the pithy but flippant style which he had not used since his "Sourmash" days. Then he engaged a public stenographer to type multiple copies of the letter, and he mailed a copy to each of the editors whose outer offices he had been haunting. Having paid the typist, he had only three dollars left of the money he had brought to New York to live upon.

In the letter, he announced to these jaded and skeptical managing editors the fact that he, Irvin S. Cobb, was probably the best newspaper man or editor the big town had ever seen, that no reporter or writer or editor then working in New York could possibly do the job half as well as Cobb could do it, and that even though Cobb had come there to raise the standards of New York journalism far above its mean state, nobody had yet demonstrated the least degree of perspicacity by hiring him.

Giving the editors one more chance to rectify a grievous oversight, Cobb remarked that he had become tired of looking at the wallpaper pattern in the outer office and that his own self-esteem "forbids me doing business with your head office boy any longer. Unless you grab me right away I will go elsewhere and leave your paper flat on its back right here in the middle of a hard summer, and your whole life hereafter will be one vast surging regret. The line forms on the left; applications considered in the order in which they are received; triflers and professional flirts save stamps. Write, wire, or call at the above address" (M, 118).[18]

In the annals of so storied a profession as American journalism, the peculiar response of tough and seasoned editors to Irvin Cobb's outlandish letter of application must surely be one of the most incongruous of episodes. Over the years, the story of that letter has been so good in the telling that it has rarely been told accurately, even though Cobb's personal account in *Myself—to Date* (117–22) is clear and uncomplicated. According to the rest of his account, he went directly to the office of the *Evening Sun* on the morning after he had mailed his letter, and there he sent in his card exactly as he had done at least a dozen times before. But on this occasion an editor came to the door and said, in effect, that if Cobb's talent as journalist matched his monumental nerve, he was the same as hired.[19] Cobb accepted instantly and went to work the next day as telegraph editor at fifteen dollars a week.

From Leg Man to Syndicated Columnist

Irvin Cobb spent a year working for the *New York Evening Sun*. At first he was dismayed to find that in the big cities—that is, in cities of the first magnitude rather than in large regional cities like Louisville—the newspapers had developed specialized methods designed to minimize the big-city obstacles of vast distances, dense populations, and crowded thoroughfares, all of which put a premium upon the need for swift and efficient communication.

He soon realized that the inviolable distinctions the city papers drew between "leg man" and "re-write man" worked against the reporter who was already skilled at getting the facts and writing the story himself. For the first time he understood the differences between specialist and general practitioner. Moreover, he saw immediately that on the New York newspapers a young reporter had to become a specialist as soon as possible if he expected to qualify as a member of the journalistic "team"—the "leg man," who was at the scene of the story, and the "re-write man," who stayed in the city room of the newspaper office to take the news by telephone.

Cobb began his New York career with three or four days of practice in rewriting material, and he did so while he was editing routine telegraph dispatches. Moreover, even in these spasmodic assignments, he did not rewrite "live" news as it came to the office from a "leg man." Instead, in the much broader sense of the term, he merely rewrote material from clippings. With a flush of self-confidence he unleashed himself by "smoking up" the liveliest and most vivid news story he could write from the bare and dispassionate clippings that were his only source. But the next morning when he read the story in the paper he found that the copy readers had excised all his finest touches. At this moment he realized that in big city shops an unproved young reporter must "stick to the plainest and most unornamental English until he is established" (*M,* 129).

Cobb's opportunity to work as an outside man came inadvertently during his fourth day of work, when an acting city editor sent him into the streets to cover an impending strike of public transportation workers. When he had enough material he went back to the newspaper office to begin writing the story himself. As he discovered almost too late, it was considered a form of professional suicide to work alone on a story, since in New York every reporter who is assigned to a story along with reporters from other papers "is in honor bound to divide with his fellows any and every legitimate item of information which comes into his possession for so long as he is detailed to the assignment."[20] Any reporter who works alone and keeps his information from the others is ostracized by the whole combine. For this reason the so-called individual "news beat" or "scoop" is mostly a newspaper myth.

A top-notch "leg man" is a highly trained specialist in oral composition and communication. He transmits his material by telephone to the "re-write man," who is equally a specialist in recording the information and in translating the rapidly spoken hints of the "leg man" into accurate, lively, and dramatic copy. Possessed of the remarkable talent for oral discourse that eventually made him one of America's most widely admired after-dinner speakers, Cobb soon mastered these techniques. Indeed, his rigorous training as a "leg man" for the *Sun* gave him his earliest professional training in the art of the oral anecdote. But he was not happy working as a "leg man." No matter how adroitly he conveyed the news by telephone, he was not doing what he did best and what he most enjoyed. He was not doing any writing at all, and more than ever he felt that he was a man with whole talents whose real powers had been somehow divided.

In the middle of the winter the *Sun* decided to create a "lobster edition," an early edition that was to come off the presses at eight o'clock in the morning instead of at ten. In deference to Cobb's broad background in editing and headlining, as well as in deference to his proved capacity to adjust himself to new responsibilities, the managing editor made him editor of the new edition.

In his job as editor of the "lobster," Cobb felt for the first time that the *Sun* had recognized his training and accomplishments. Better still, he found in his new position exactly the right opportunity to capitalize upon his extraordinary command of written language and his penchant for wandering in odd corners of the city.

Coming to work at two o'clock in the morning, he could observe regularly the furtive nether-world of night dwellers, whose peculiar half-lives he but dimly understood because his work had prevented his being a night creature. Every morning he occupied the streets along with "the outcast, the criminal, and the homeless, the roisterer, the waster and the profligate—the classes who never work and the classes who never quit working.[21] Because there was no "lobster edition" on Sundays, he spent most of his Saturday nights in the streets, wandering through the small hours of the morning among the street people.

At about three o'clock one morning, a diligent "leg man" called in a sensational story about a murder that had just occurred in a sordid dive that Cobb recognized from a recent visit. So he wrote the story himself instead of giving it to the "re-write" man. Absorbed in his firsthand impressions of the scene, he loaded the story with what he considered "local color." Moreover, he edited the proofs himself, so that nothing could be cut out by the regular copy readers. For the first time, a news story that was pure, spontaneous, undiluted Cobb had reached the pages of a New York newspaper. The effect was sensational. As one writer has explained, "He wrote in a way that New York had not been accustomed to and his work attracted attention."[22]

For the time being, Cobb refused offers of employment from two other New York newspapers whose editors had read the story of the Tenderloin murder. He knew that he had truly arrived as a top-flight New York journalist when his paper sent him on a special assignment to cover a peace conference being held in Portsmouth, New Hampshire. This was an international conclave whose aim was to establish the peace terms of a recent war between Russia and Japan.

A large corps of correspondents from major cities was covering the conference. As a matter of habit, these reporters appear to have informally clustered into a loose-knit counterpart of the standard big-city news combine. They all worked together, and except for some differences in the style and organization of their pieces, all newspaper accounts of the conference proceedings were alike.

Cobb perceived that, by virtue of this regular flow of standard reports concerning the business of the conference, the news-reading public was amply informed by those who were already on the job. To the representative of the *Sun,* who had cut his professional teeth on the writing of ever-popular "personals" in Paducah, and to that same reporter who had garnered a faithful following of readers in Louisville by giving them a "Sourmash" column of wry observations upon human behavior, the conference at Portsmouth offered an opportunity to depict an important historical event from a point of view neglected by the battery of professional newsmen.

Instead of taking his place among the other correspondents, Cobb worked alone and obtained all his information by methods he had invented for himself. He went directly "behind the scenes" of the conference. He haunted the restaurants, the hotel lobbies, the cloakrooms, the anterooms—wherever official conference delegates came together to talk with each other unguardedly. He observed every least revealing gesture and action that shed light upon the character or motives of the individual men who in only a few hours would become key figures in some crucial decision. Becoming acquainted with several delegates or their attachés, and exercising the utmost discretion in the use of information, he was able to take part in their informal airings of issues both public and private.

Under the title "Making Peace at Portsmouth," Cobb's best articles were often purely anecdotal. They revealed through small and seemingly irrelevant incidents the dramatic contrasts in temperament, ethnic differences, and personal idiosyncracies of men whose decisions ruled the conference but who came alive, as people, only in the columns Cobb sent back to the *Sun.* These articles "had more to do with the rise and fall of Russian whiskers and Japanese politeness than they did with the facts of the peace conference,"[23] observes John Wilson Townsend. And Robert H. Davis says, "There wasn't a single fact in the entire series, and yet *The Sun* syndicated these stories throughout the United States. All they possessed was I-N-D-I-V-I-D-U-A-L-I-T-Y."[24]

As a by-line to this syndicated series of articles, the name of Irvin S. Cobb became familiar to people all over America. At the same time, as a special feature writer, he could command a premium salary from almost any New York newspaper. He received nearly half a dozen tempting offers from New York editors as soon as he was back at his desk in the office of the *Sun.* For a short time he politely declined these offers, but a proposal by the *Evening and Sunday World* proved irresistible.

The *World*: School for a Free-Lance

For a New York City reporter in 1905, and even for a special feature writer of that era, an offer of sixty-five dollars a week was the kind of compliment that transcended lesser loyalties. Moreover, under the leadership of men like Chapin and Van Hamm, the *World* was on the threshold of creating one of the brilliant dynasties in American journalism. It brought together within the next twenty years the talents of such distinguished journalists and critics as Deems Taylor, Laurence Stallings, Harry Hansen, William Bolitho, Franklin P. Adams, and Alexander Woollcott. Of this era Irvin Cobb was a distinguished pioneer.

According to a *Newsweek* capsule, "On the *World,* Cobb became one of the top reporters of his day. He covered the White House wedding of Alice Roosevelt Longworth. On the trial of Harry K. Thaw for the murder of Stanford White, the noted architect, Cobb poured 600,000 words from the courtroom."[25] In the six years of his tenure he enjoyed many other triumphs as well.

During his years on the *World* he brought his wife and baby daughter to New York. These were also the years when he lost his resemblance to the Paducah lad called "Shriv'ly" or "Bonesey" and acquired instead the dimensions of the genial fat man who would soon be hailed as one of America's leading humorists. He was always ready to laugh with others at the spectacle of his own fatness and at his own rationalizing. "For every added pound an added excuse, for each multiplying inch at the waistline a new plea in abatement to be set up in the mind," he wrote. "I see the truth of it now. When you start getting fat you start getting fatuous."[26]

Yet his imposing figure seems always to have been an advantage rather than a handicap. Indeed, his stature as a humorist and as a fiction writer was frequently measured in terms of his physical dimensions. Ellis Parker Butler thought so when he said of Cobb's humorous columns in the *World:* "It was hard and continuous work and wore him down until he was hardly the size of two ordinary men, and the strain on his reservoir of humor was so great that some nights his dab of stuff was only twice as funny as anything else published that day."[27]

By the time Cobb left the *World* to become a full-time writer of fiction and occasional pieces for the magazines, he was drawing a salary of a hundred and sixty-five dollars a week as a self-styled "newspaper minion."[28] Some knowledgeable critics have contended that, at that time and on this salary, Irvin Cobb was the highest-paid evening newspaper reporter in the world.

Incredible Truth

For the rest of his life Cobb regarded himself primarily as a professional journalist. To him, journalism was the essential training ground for all good writing. "Newspaper work—that's the answer," he once wrote. "That's where you'll find out if you have a writer in you. And if you have a writer in you, that's where you'll become one."[29] He insisted that the art of good reporting is a high challenge to the best of writers, and that some of the world's most memorable writing has been achieved by the eyewitness reporter.

In order to demonstrate the dramatic power and the universal appeal of the best eyewitness reporting, Cobb published a book titled *Incredible Truth* (1931). A remarkable venture, *Incredible Truth* is an early experiment in the writing of history mostly in the present tense, much as television programs have dramatized important historical events under such titles as "You Are There." *Incredible Truth,* however, is a compendium of eyewitness reports by historical personages who are closely connected with if not participants in historical events. These eyewitnesses are not historians but "active journalists on the job" (x). In selecting his material, Cobb searched for "graphic, vivid, and vigorous first-person, present-tense annals of historic events in our own country and in older countries as well; in this generation and in the generations before us" (x). Above all, Cobb sought eyewitness accounts that make for "stirring reading" (219).

Of all Cobb's books, *Incredible Truth* is the most convincing demonstration of Cobb's omnivorous reading, his comprehensive mind, and his astounding memory. Ranging freely over the events of ancient and modern history, he selects only the most dramatic and memorable eyewitness accounts his memory can produce. Moreover, he uses stringent editorial restraint in isolating only the essential passage or passages from accounts that are often forbiddingly extensive. In order to restrict the first-person account to passages that are seldom longer than six or eight pages, he writes his own preliminary and sometimes linking comments, in which he gives the historical backgrounds, introduces historical personages, and draws a perspective full of minute detail that might impress even specialized scholars. The result is that

Cobb manages to humanize people who would otherwise remain dim and distant figures in the standard history books.

Throughout his career as a writer Irvin Cobb was conscious of his debt to the long history of the reportorial craft. Even in the day of yellow journalism, even "in the day of the studhorse headline; the day when the more private a man's affairs might be the more public they were made,"[30] Cobb was aware of the historical necessity of his calling. "When a big story broke and no one asked me to cover it," he once said, "why, I'd borrow a police card and cover it for myself."[31]

Chapter Three
Funny Glasses

Cobb had spent only fifteen months with the *Sun* before he moved next door to the *World,* where he was to spend the next six years. During this period—the longest he ever spent with a single newspaper—his output and his total salary depended upon his ingenuity in maintaining one or another of six different humorous columns. These were "New York Through Funny Glasses," "The Hotel Clerk," "Live Talks with Dead Ones," "The Gotham Geography," "The Diary of Noah," and "The Browse Brothers—Hiram and Loerum." Except for "New York Through Funny Glasses," which ran four or five years as a daily feature, these were half-page illustrated weekly features written for the Sunday edition of the *World.*

In his job on the *New York World,* Irvin Cobb was a nationally known "personality" newspaperman, and when he acquired this position, he entered irretrievably upon his lifelong career as one of America's leading humorists. Though his regular job consisted of the standard "bread and butter" assignments from which he earned his base salary, his reputation came from extra jobs of writing for which he was paid separately. Already well known for his work on the *Sun,* he was now prepared to capitalize upon his own idiosyncracies. Moreover, as a pioneer in an astonishing line of "personality" columnists and feature writers that followed him to the *World* in the next two decades, Irvin Cobb succeeded better than he probably had any reason to hope.

Most of his regular staff assignments had nothing to do with "personality" material nor with humorous composition. "I was a reasonably busy person," he later told Thomas Masson. "I was a reporter, a rewrite man, and at intervals a staff correspondent on out-of-town assignments. I covered the two Thaw trials and probably a dozen other big criminal cases. Between times I wrote an average of three satirical or supposedly humorous signed articles a week for the magazine page of the *Evening World* and contributed special articles to the *Sunday World.*"[1] The key phrase in this quotation is "between times," for he regarded his prolific humorous writing as a sideline.

"New York Through Funny Glasses"

From the "funny stuff" and the "personals" of the old Paducah paper to the sophisticated columns of the *New York World* seems a long leap. Yet almost every previous phase of Irvin Cobb's career as newspaperman had prepared him for the journalistic post that he occupied by the middle of the summer in 1908. Now his material was published nationally by the syndicated press, and he was soon to be known nationwide as the top humorist of the day among New York journalists. He was to occupy this position for several years—until by his own admission every newspaper had acquired one or more "personality" columnists. "Now newspapers have so many columnists," said Cobb in 1941, "that . . . average news stories are merely the solder which binds the joints between the columns" (*EL,* 264).

During his first years on the *World,* however, Cobb was still one of the few journalists who formed a vanguard for the kind of writing that was first made popular by Eugene Field's famous "Sharps and Flats" column in Chicago in the 1880s and 1890s—a feature that has become known as the first "modern" newspaper column. In 1908, Cobb was still a pioneer in this special journalistic form.

His first column for the *World* was a feature he wrote on the average of two or three times a week for the regular columns of the daily issues of the paper. It appeared originally as "New York Through Funny Glasses," though by the middle of the summer in 1908 Cobb had changed the standard spelling of "through" to "thro'." The new spelling made no difference in the pronunciation, but it pleased Cobb's eye because it was quaintly colloquial. The "funny glasses" were usually characterized as two men, one named "Hi Glasses," a typical New Yorker, and "Green Glasses," an unsophisticated resident of some other part of the country. Cobb frequently wrote the column in the form of a letter from "Hi Glasses" to "Green Glasses," informing the latter of the various "goings on" in the big city of New York. The column was seldom longer than five hundred words, though it occupied extra space in column inches because it carried a small full-face photograph of Cobb and, usually, one or two small illustrative cartoons in the daily magazine and story section of the *World.* Cobb maintained the column for several years before giving it up in favor of the more advantageous half-page columns in the Sunday magazine section.

As the title suggests, "New York Through Funny Glasses" was intended as a humorous inside view of daily life in New York City. Typical of "Funny Glasses" is the column of 3 July 1908, which is Cobb's Fourth of July commentary for that year. Written as one of the letters of Hi Glasses to Green Glasses, it relates in a matter-of-fact tone the early-morning explosion of a giant firecracker which removed "most of the outer garments and several fingers of a bright lad residing next door." Another emblem of the day is a father's demonstration of a whistling bomb that surrounds him and his sons with smoke-trails, "giving a realistic off-hand imitation of that well-known statuary group . . . , showing the late Mr. Laocoon and his sons Egbert and Henry J. Laocoon, Jr., of Athens, Greece, who went into the snake charming business and never entirely recovered from it."

Another example of Cobb's topical and local humor appears in the "Funny Glasses" column of 11 July 1908. Here Hi Glasses tells Green Glasses that the "Broadway coterie" has entered into the local activity of "organizing movements for the uplift of mankind." The best of the organizations is "the society for the Canning of Ancient Wheezes," whose members have agreed to prohibit the use of seven old wheezes. Most of the wheezes are highly topical and local, such as references to the governor's whiskers, to the directoire or sheath skirt, and to New York as a summer resort.

From time to time Cobb uses "Funny Glasses" to pretend that he is another kind of columnist, as for instance when he pretends to be a drama critic in the "Funny Glasses" column of 18 July 1908. In this column he drops all pretense that the column consists of a letter in any form. Instead he writes as a local drama critic, using the names of real playwrights like Clyde Fitch or other names so close to real as to leave no doubt at all of the reference, as in this remark that is obviously aimed at Eva Tanguay: "Miss Ever Tankway, billed as the Gallus Girl, sings, 'I Don't Care, if I Did I Couldn't Do It,' shedding half a pound of real human hair at every performance." He also refers to a production by "the new school of systematic-osteopathic-psychopathic-allopathic dramas" at the "Clinical Theatre." At the end he quotes a group of egregiously bad reviews and shows how a press agent selects words and phrases from them to make a production appear to be a hit.

In the "Funny Glasses" column of 25 July 1908, Cobb uses a letter from Hi Glasses to remark upon the behavior of the British at the Olympic games currently being held in England. In a typical column of its kind, Cobb shows that, from the British point of view, an American athlete should be disqualified for three reasons: "First—He beat an Englishman. Second—He is an American. Third—Same as number 2 only harder."

The Hotel Clerk Series

At the time when Cobb was writing the "Funny Glasses" series, he also began writing his first weekly series for the *Sunday World*. This series consisted of a half-page column—about 2,000 words of composition and at least one large illustration—that appeared every Sunday in the magazine section. Cobb never missed doing an installment of the series, even though it was a purely optional opportunity.

The ingenious idea behind "The Hotel Clerk" series is that, during the lagging hours of the night shift, the clerks in the big New York hotels have large amounts of time with nothing to do except to carry on conversations with other hotel employees. In "The Hotel Clerk," Cobb portrays the head clerk of the Hotel St. Reckless as conversing upon the topics of the day with the house detective, whom the clerk familiarly calls "Larry," or with the head bellboy, even more familiarly called "Hops." As the employee highest in professional station and therefore presumably most knowledgeable, the head clerk provides the main topics of the conversations, with the house detective or the bellboy merely injecting reactive commentaries or asking questions. For this reason the title of the column is sometimes altered slightly to read "The Hotel Clerk Says—."

As in the daily "Funny Glasses" series, the subjects for the Sunday column were limited only by questions of whether the remarks concerned matters of immediate interest to New Yorkers. But Cobb usually managed to find subjects that were equally of interest to the country at large. Therefore the syndicated nationwide distribution of the columns found interested readers wherever the columns appeared.

As in the "Funny Glasses" series, "The Hotel Clerk" series never lets a major holiday go by without a corresponding number in the series. On Sunday, 24 November 1907, for instance, Cobb provides an installment titled "Thanksgiving in New York—As the Hotel Clerk Sees It." This number opens with the house detective opining that he does not have much to be thankful about for the coming Thanksgiving holiday. His remark elicits from the hotel clerk a dissertation upon the things that people currently seem to be thankful for. He provides a discussion of the pilgrims, saying, "The Pilgrim Father never lost the

habit of being thankful." But concerning "legal" holidays, he says that
there are none, since "the legal profession don't deserve one; and what's
more, it ain't got time to take one, now that the divorce business is
looking up the way it is." As for getting home for the holiday, the
head clerk insists that he is "one of several hundred thousand parties
in this town that are always going to go home for Thanksgiving or
Christmas but never do it on account of not being able to get there on
a Broadway car without taking a transfer."

From one holiday season to the next, Cobb was not above using the
good things he had said in one column to spice up the same column a
year later. The Fourth of July number of "The Hotel Clerk" on 28 June
1908, for instance, used most of the wheezes he had already used in
the "Funny Glasses" number the year before. Indeed, to fill up his
2,000 words of space he reused so much material that one wonders
why he did not tire his readers with the belaboring of references to
blown-off fingers and other forms of dismemberment from the use of
fireworks. But in the current column he adds the character of a Mr.
Framingham, who is a dedicated traditional observer of the Fourth of
July and who is the specific person who suffers the traditional misfor-
tunes. This device seemed to satisfy Cobb's readers that this version of
"'It'll be a Glorious Fourth if We Live Through It,' Says the Hotel
Clerk" is really a different column from the "Funny Glasses" installment of the year before.

Cobb never seemed to run out of topical subjects that were of interest to New Yorkers and to the country at large. On 14 June 1908, for
instance, he addresses himself to the perennially interesting aspiration
of young people to become famous as Broadway stars. The head bell
boy at the St. Reckless has a sister, Mame, who plans to go on the
stage. First she is going to choose a "stage name"; then she will go to
the big stage managers, "and the one that offers her the most money,
she'll take him." But melodramas are not refined enough for her. So
she plans to go into musicals because the girls wear "swell regalia" and
do not have much to do, and they "snag off some splendid young Yale
feller that's got a millionaire for a father."

Cobb also writes an installment on the speedy and expeditious jury
trial system in New Jersey. This system conveniently finds all prisoners
guilty and sends them to be hanged. Indeed, says Cobb, "about the
only thing a man could feel safe in committing in New Jersey was
suicide," compared with New York, where, "we hang nobody that's
anybody and rarely ever anybody that's nobody." Moreover, in New

York a jury sometimes sets a prisoner free, depriving him of the comforts of his cell with all the goodies people bring. Then he "gets a job writing for the magazines and builds him a villa over on Long Island and is looked up to." Anyway, concludes the head clerk, "in New York, being innocent is a crime."

On 19 July 1908, there is a typical "Hotel Clerk" number in which the house detective and the head clerk consider whether the Northern and Southern Civil War veterans could hold a combined meeting without "bustin' up in a row." Says the head clerk, "They kept fairly steady company for four years once on a stretch and parted with mutual reluctance even then."

The installment of 6 February 1910 contains a boxed announcement that the next week "Mr. Cobb will begin a new series of humorous papers under the general title of 'Live Talks with Dead Ones.' The 'dead ones' are famous personages of the past whom Mr. Cobb will interview in the interest of his readers." The first interview of the new series was to be a talk with St. Valentine for the Valentine's Day issue of the *Sunday World*.

"Live Talks with Dead Ones"

The first installment of the new humorous series by Cobb is introduced by another boxed announcement explaining that Cobb's interview with St. Valentine is the first number of a series that replaces the "whimsical philosophy" of the Hotel Clerk. There is also an announcement that the second number of the series will consist of an interview with "Miss Terpsichore Muse, of the Muse Sisters, on Dancing."

In the St. Valentine interview, the reporter goes at first to the wrong house and finds the wrong St. Valentine—the one "who choked to death on a fishbone in the second century." But Cobb finds the real St. Valentine only a few doors away. The saint converses in modern idiom but seems altogether unaware of the modern St. Valentine's Day customs. He is particularly upset to know that on his day people customarily send "a printed atrocity" in a plain envelope to peculiar folk or to those whom one dislikes—in the name of "comics." The upshot of the interview is that Cobb has to inform the venerable saint that "In your time, sir, and for some time subsequent, I believe, all the world loved a lover; now all the world loves to laugh at one."

After his promised interview with Miss Terpsichore Muse as the second number of "Live Talks," Cobb goes to Shakespeare for his third installment. Informed by Cobb that in the modern theater Shakespeare seems to be a "back number," Shakespeare admits that in his attempts to talk with local theater managers he has been able to see only the office boys. The bard observes that "realism is the keynote" and that one must do "the problem play, a form of drama that treats a particularly nasty subject in a particularly nasty, unparticular way." He admits, however, that some things have not changed. For instance, "Making an exit a villainess pauses at the door and looks back meaningly, whether she means anything or not—which was a favorite by-play with all the villainesses that ever worked for me."

In the "Live Talks" series Cobb has an interview (17 April 1910) with Edgar Allan Poe, whom he depicts as sitting with his live crow, "Nevermore," on his shoulder, and as receiving the news that he has at last been admitted among the American immortals. "Having had me on probation all these years," muses Poe, "the worthy gentlemen have decided that I'm sobered up sufficiently to be allowed in a select society." There is also a typical interview (1 May 1910) with Spartacus the Gladiator, who denies that he ever made a famous speech to the gladiators. "The real fighting persons, like U. S. Grant and Brian Boru and me and others," contends Spartacus, "were always too busy slamming knockouts across to be wasting time thinking up eloquent remarks for campaign and after-dinner purposes."

Each of Cobb's columns for the *World* allowed him to see contemporary society from a slightly different angle and to comment upon an endless variety of popular subjects, each with its current appeal for an audience that grew steadily larger. For the most part his ingenuity was so rich that he covered almost every topic of the day, and most of his readers found even the repetitive material entertaining. Soon he realized that much of his material was suitable for publication in the "slick" magazines. This discovery encouraged him to start "tailoring" his essays and articles to the requirements of the magazines, and during his last two or three years with the *World* he was writing regularly for the "slick" periodicals. From this point, Irvin Cobb's career spread in several directions at once, though his reading public always persisted in regarding him as foremost a humorous writer.

The Corpulent Comic

As a humorist, Irvin Cobb had a most valuable physical asset—his own considerable corpulence. His plumpness came upon him quickly over a period of months after he had gone to work for the *World,* and except that he had a fondness for good if not gourmet food, this rapid gain in weight is not easily explainable. According to "Buff" Cobb, "One day he was a long, lean, Gary-Cooper-legged boy, the next a fat man."[2] At any rate, for the sake of his readers he lost no time in projecting himself in the role of "the comic fat man in essays for the *Saturday Evening Post*"[3] and many other magazines.

Soon Cobb became known the country over as the epitome of the funny fat man, whose corpulence not only gets him into all sorts of amusing trouble but also as one who is able to make situations all the funnier because an excessively fat man is the butt of the joke. For Cobb, funny articles and stories about his corpulence became a staple source of income. Indeed, as one writer remarks, "No other genius has so successfully lived on his fat."[4]

One of the earliest and most widely read exploitations of Cobb's corpulence appears in *Cobb's Anatomy* (1912). Though the *Anatomy* is not devoted entirely to the attributes of the fat person, its first section—on "Tummies"—is a thoroughgoing exploitation of the embarrassing corpulence of the fat person. By implication, the other sections of the book—"Teeth," "Hair," "Hands and Feet"—are also parts of the anatomy of the same fat person whose oversize "tummy" is the subject of the opening section.

The initial "thesis" of *Cobb's Anatomy,* which is a profusely illustrated book of 141 pages, is that the world accords all its best things to the man with a slender physique. "The fat man is the universal goat; he is humanity's standing joke. When a man gets a stomach his troubles begin" (9). Not only do other people find the fat man funny, says Cobb, but the fat man is expected to consider himself funny. And if he is to be consistently funny, he cannot possibly be romantic or sentimental. "It is all right for a giraffe to be sentimental," he declares, "but not a hippopotamus" (11). His conclusion is that "of all the ills the flesh is heir to, the worst is the flesh itself" (28).

As for teeth, says Cobb, one of the pleasantest things about birth is that we are born without any teeth, and "we are generally fairly well content with life until teeth begin to come" (36). But we do not have them long until we begin to lose them, "and after awhile, they are all gone and our face folds up on us like a crush hat or a concertina and from our brow to our chin we don't look much more than a third as long as we used to look" (40). Concerning the hair, one goes along all right until "all of a sudden you wake up to the realization that your head is working its way up through the hair" (100), and when "only about two thirds of it is gone your head looks like a great auk's egg in a snug nest" (101). As for hands, every boy wishes he could have an extra pair for the various employments he puts them to, except when they must be washed or when they are particularly noticeable in public gatherings. The feet are even more troublesome, since they "are proverbially ungrateful. You do for them and they do you" (139). All this is an intimate form of anatomical humor, and in *Cobb's Anatomy* the author fully capitalizes upon it.

One closely related source of this humor is the corpulent person's love of food. In this sense, *Cobb's Bill of Fare* (1913) belongs with *Cobb's Anatomy* as part of the comedy of corpulence. The comparative value of good food is suggested on the cover of this little book, where a logo or a large seal shows a corpulent person seated at a table surrounded in turn by symbols of art, music, sports, and "vittles." This aspect of Cobb's corpulence is given a fine tribute by Sara Smith Campbell in "The Clown Prince of Gourmets,"[5] wherein the author details some of Cobb's favorite "down yonder" recipes, most of them remembered from his boyhood days in Paducah.

In other sections of *Cobb's Bill of Fare,* the author uses for comic purposes his own "common man" attitude toward such "highbrow" subjects as music and art. "All I ask of a picture is that it shall look like something," he says, "and all I expect of music is that it shall sound like something" (81).

One of Cobb's most popular exploitations of his own corpulence is an article titled "The Great Reduction," which appeared in the *Saturday Evening Post* on 16 July 1921. This piece amused Cobb's readers by explaining not only how a person becomes fat but also how one might attempt to reduce. Most amusing are the various ways by which the fat person persuades himself that he is not really fat and that certain forms of pleasant but purposeless exercise will result in a lessening of weight. Invariably, of course, an increase of appetite defeats this purpose.

In a second installment Cobb endeavors once more to lose weight. After consulting physicians whose theories all disagree with each other, Cobb finds his own diet, and it works. After backsliding a time or two, he holds to the diet and at last finds that he has gone from two hundred and thirty-six pounds to one hundred and ninety-seven. He hopes eventually to take off exactly one third of his former weight.

Under the title *One Third Off,* the two articles were published in a single volume in 1921.

The Born Loser

Despite his being "bulky in spots" as he once described himself, Irvin Cobb had a good deal of success in portraying himself as the so-called "little man." In American humor, the "little man" is the consistent "loser," and Cobb is a pioneer in this field. A few decades later it was perfected by Robert Benchley, who projected an image of himself as the world's prize scapegoat. In American literature, Cobb shares with Benchley the role of the "bumbler upset by technology, mass media, and mass-man."[6]

In his role as the "little man" Cobb wrote the most widely read and the most highly praised humorous piece of his career—an eight thousand word familiar essay titled "Speaking of Operations—." Based upon Cobb's hospital sojourn in the spring of 1915, "Speaking of Operations—" first appeared in the *Saturday Evening Post* of 6 November 1915. The reaction of readers was so favorable and so nearly universal that Cobb's publisher, George Doran, lost no time in issuing it as a sixty-four-page volume illustrated by Tony Sarg. In only a few years the little book sold more than a half million copies, and eventually it was translated into nearly a dozen foreign languages. The "hospital edition" has been widely read in doctors' offices and hospital waiting rooms all over America. In 1929 it was included in *Irvin Cobb at His Best.*

Beginning the essay with a consideration of popular topics of conversation, Cobb reaches the conclusion that "the king of all topics is operations," since the teller "is not only the hero of the tale but the rest of the cast and the stage setting as well" (14). Cobb then relates his own experiences with doctors, and particularly with specialists, whose methods he deplores. He says of them that "any time Dr. Y ventured below the throat he was out of bounds and liable to be penalized" (20).

Of his operation and his subsequent term of recovery at "St. Germicide's" hospital, Cobb provides ample and concrete detail. Though he had planned to be cavalier and carefree on his way into the operating room, he felt "instinctively . . . that humor was out of place here" (41). After the operation, one of his first sensations was that "those doctors had not left anything inside of me except the accoustics" (47), and later, when he had regained his appetite, they let him "suck a little glass thermometer, but there is not much nourishment, really, in thermometers" (48). He then provides a mock history of medicine, beginning with medieval times and coming to the time when Cobb wrote the piece. Along the way he considers the family doctor of his childhood, who apparently chose all his medicines "on the principle that unless a drug tasted like the very dickens it couldn't possibly do you any good" (54). Having recovered, however, Cobb finds himself able to be more lenient toward the average physician, saying, "He is with us when we come into the world and with us when we go out of it, oftentimes lending a helping hand on both occasions" (57).

The striking thing about this essay is its unflagging modernity. After sixty years of seeming progress in medical techniques and hospital procedures the essay remains almost as relevant as it was when Cobb wrote it in 1915. Though some of the hospital equipment is outdated, in its essence the experience remains fresh. Cobb's experiences as a surgery patient are recognizable, universally applicable to general experience, and thoroughly amusing. Moreover, this essay is the source of one of the most quotable of quotations in American literature—"I was not having any more privacy in that hospital than a goldfish" (38). Habitually shortened to simply "no more privacy than a goldfish," this quotation remains one of the most venerable clichés in the English language.

In the role of the born loser, Cobb also wrote *The Abandoned Farmers*,[8] which is an account of Cobb's attempts to acquire an abandoned farm in Connecticut during the time when it was a vogue among affluent city people to seek a haven from hectic city life. Yearning to get back to the land, the Cobbs joined the stampede, and eventually they built the country home which they called "Rebel Ridge."

Along the way, however, Cobb has a complicated series of misadventures with farm owners, real estate men, confidence artists, tradesmen, artisans, handy men, and neighbors. At first it seems to the Cobbs a simple matter to buy an abandoned farm. One simply finds a farm for sale within easy commuting distance of the city, and one purchases the property. But after fruitlessly touring the countryside, Cobb at last resorts to a desperate but comical ploy. Seeing a place he likes, he demands to know when the owner plans to abandon the premises. The owner concludes that Cobb must be a lunatic.

The trouble with living in New York, says Cobb, is that the teeming millions of people "are constantly engaged in going somewhere in such a hurry. Nearly always the place where they are going lies in the opposite direction from the place where you are going" (60). These conditions make a person think "of peaceful fields and burdened orchards, and kind-faced cows standing knee-deep in purling brooks, and bosky dells and sylvan glades" (61). As a last resort he buys some sylvan property and lives in a tent while building his own country home out of brick, tile, slate, and original beams from an abandoned brickyard nearby. The result is a beautiful home that matches the landscape. But he is cheated and defrauded at every stage of the project.

The Happy Wanderer: Foreign Travel

Among Cobb's most successful humorous pieces are several books, articles, and essays that can be loosely categorized as literature of travel. In a short but witty essay called "Travel"[9] he toys with the notion that the ideal mode of travel is to stay at home and visit distant lands only by means of travel folders and the inspired imagination. For everybody except the exceedingly wealthy, it seems to Cobb, travel is so expensive and so full of inconvenience as to make it hardly worth while.

He considers all the unglamorous aspects of famous biblical journeys like those of Noah and the Children of Israel. Even Charles Dickens's exuberant accounts of travels over the English countryside, says Cobb, could not altogether conceal the inconveniences of stage-coach travel. Then he details a few things that confirmed travelers prefer to forget after every excursion—expensive hotels, glum ticket agents, upper berths in sleeping cars, bad food, dining-car cocktails that are like swallowing Roman candles, and cigars that taste like a burning rag carpet.

In his most widely read travel book, *Europe Revised,* Cobb followed the path that Mark Twain had blazed with *Innocents Abroad* in 1869. Twain had departed from the usual travel-book format by seeking "to suggest to the reader how *he* would be likely to see Europe and the East if he looked at them with his own eyes instead of the eyes of those who traveled in those countries before him."[10] Twain had accomplished this purpose by providing a broadly personalized and subjective account of all that he saw and did on his trip to Europe and the Near East in 1867. Upon its appearance his large two-volume account became almost instantly the most widely read travel book in America.

When Irvin Cobb sailed for Europe on the *Lusitania* in 1913, he had decided to follow Twain's lead in writing a purely personal and subjective account of his travels. In the early spring of 1914 he published in the *Saturday Evening Post* eleven installments of his account under the title of "An American Vandal." These installments proved so successful that within two months Cobb expanded them into a full-sized travel book which George Doran issued under the title of *Europe Revised*. It was immediately accepted by readers and critics as a worthy successor to *Innocents Abroad*, and in that later era it was almost as widely read.

Europe Revised is an even more whimsical account of foreign travel than Twain's book is. Assuming the role of the typical middle-class American tourist, Cobb judges everything according to his tastes, and he successfully reflects the likes and dislikes of the average American who finds himself suddenly in a foreign land. In this book, Cobb makes no attempt to record "facts," as the standard guide books have usually done. Indeed, he writes, "it occurred to me that possibly there might be room for a guidebook on foreign travel which would not have a single indubitable fact concealed anywhere about its person."[11]

The book is an account of Cobb's three months' sojourn in London, Paris, Berlin, Rome, Naples, Venice, and Pompeii. Though he suffers from the general epidemic of seasickness aboard the ship, he prefers to accept the steward's diplomatic suggestion that, unlike the others, he merely suffers from something called "climate fever."

In London he expects to find a thick fog, but there is none. When he leaves Paris for Rome, he finds that he is expected to tip every employee of the hotel. Then he travels through Rome, Naples, Venice, the Austrian Tyrol, and into Germany, getting glimpses of native life and customs in each place.

In a section on American food versus European food, American cuisine is the winner by a wide margin. According to Cobb, the French diet is strictly *poulet rôti* (roast chicken) and veal. So unvarying is this menu as to force one to conclude that "according to the French version of the story of the Flood, only two animals emerged from the Ark when the waters receded—one was an immature hen and the other was an adolescent calf" (157).

In a section called "Modes of the Moment," Cobb writes of fashions in English clothing. He relates his experience in having himself fitted for an English raincoat and a pair of English knee britches. The tailor "seemed to labor under the impression that I was going to use my raincoat for holding large public assemblies or social gatherings in"

(180), and his knee breeches "appeared to be constructed for cargo rather than speed" (185).

In a section comparing the military uniforms of various nationalities, Cobb stands for a considerable time staring at the midsection of a tall British footguard outside Buckingham Palace. He wants to know whether the tall guard "had any human emotions." But after a long time during which the guard gives no sign of life or consciousness whatever, Cobb goes away "feeling all wriggly" (197).

He complains about the spirit of "small, mean graft" that prevails in every hostelry, every restaurant, every place of business on the Continent. He is particularly disillusioned by those who claim to be guides but who spend most of their time steering the tourist into various shops in order to get a commission upon the sales. Large numbers of guides claim to have served as the personal guide for Mark Twain on one or another of his European tours, all the way back to the time, many years before, when Twain was gathering material for his travel book, *Innocents Abroad.*

In Rome, says Cobb, "I saw ruins until I was one myself," and though he is thoroughly impressed by the excavations at Pompeii, he is disappointed at finding no evidence at all of the famous soldier whom Mark Twain had praised for staying at his post until he was buried in the ashes of Vesuvius.

A decade and a half later, Cobb made a memorable tour of South America and recorded his impressions in *Both Sides of the Street* (1930), a book he prefers to call a "journal" or a "sketch book" rather than a guide book. Keenly aware that the continents of North and South America are close neighbors "on both sides of the street," Cobb sets out on his journey convinced that "South America is the land of the future. It is the one land which not yet has been fully explored for sightseeing purposes nor completely exploited for commerce, but for the most part remains an unspoiled land, still awaiting the peak of its development . . . , still abounding in glamour and color and novelty for the romantically inclined and the sportsman" (4–5).

Accompanied by his good friends Will Hogg and Dean Palmer, Cobb goes down the West coast of South America, crosses the Andes, and travels up the East Coast, visiting in succession Panama, Peru, Chile, Argentina, Uruguay, and Brazil. In his avowed attempt to "rediscover South America" (43) Cobb stays in each of the major South American cities long enough to get the special "feel" of the South American cultures and to understand the peculiarities of the people.

In Lima he discovers that "Mañana-land no longer is content to drowse in the sunshine" (63), and as early as 1929 he predicts the eventual construction of the Pan-American highway (58), which was actually coming to completion fifty years later. In transit to Argentina, Cobb finds that going "out of Chile into the Argentine is rather like going at one jump from Southern California to western Nebraska by way of the Grand Cañon, the Royal Gorge, Yellowstone Park or what have you" (94). In the chapter on Uruguay, Cobb compares the major South American countries with certain states of the United States. "I think I'd probably call Uruguay the Massachusetts of South America," he writes, "just as I'd call Brazil its Florida, and Chile, potentially speaking, its Pennsylvania, and the Argentine its Nebraska" (118).

Cobb ends the account of his South American trip with this prediction: "If Europe is finished, if yesterday belongs to Europe, and if today is still North America's day, then surely the opportunities and the promises of tomorrow are the heritage of South America" (158).

In a separate section titled "The Folks Across the Way," Cobb includes three essays concerning foreign travel. The first of these, "To Be Taken Before Sailing," consists largely of advice to prospective travelers from the United States. The second is "The Man Who Broke the Bunk at Monte Carlo." Resolving to write only for a worthy purpose, Cobb makes it clear that he plans to expose Monte Carlo as "the saddest, the dreariest, the most sordid, most depressing conglomerate of human greed, human callousness, bad taste and hopelessness" (194) that he has ever seen. "This Hands across the Sea Stuff," the last of the little travel essays in *Both Sides of the Street,* is largely a series of anecdotes demonstrating Cobb's thesis that the "hands across the sea" are of two general types: "the hands that are held open with the fingers eagerly clutching . . . to receive the millions upon millions of American dollars which annually we bestow upon European shopkeepers and European innkeepers; and the hands . . . that behind our backs are clenched into hard and angered fists for expression of a profound disapprobation of American tourists" (216). But, says Cobb, these fists do not appear until after Americans have spent their money.

Eating in Two or Three Languages (1919) is a lighthearted essay upon Cobb's gustatory experiences in England and France during his World War I tour as a foreign correspondent. Even the title is a spoof, the "two or three languages" turning out to consist of "English, bad French, and profane" (47). Otherwise the little illustrated book is a narrative of Cobb's thwarted attempts to find tolerable food in English and French restaurants that have been forced to adjust their menus to wartime rationing regulations. In despair, Cobb turns to the private kitchens of the provincial French, where he finds the food so remarkably and uniformly good that, no matter what might have gone into the pot, "the flavor of the delectable broth cured us of any inclinations to make investigation as to the former stations in life of its basic constituents" (58).

The Happy Wanderer: Domestic Travel

During the winter of 1913–14 Cobb toured the American Southwest and California, and in the summer of 1914 George Doran issued Cobb's account of the trip under the title of *Roughing It Deluxe,* a richly descriptive and prodigally illustrated travel narrative of a visit to the Grand Canyon and Southern California.

The first two sections of the book, "A Pilgrim Canonized" and "Rabid and His Friends," deal with the Grand Canyon. Though Cobb insists that the awesome beauty of the canyon is impossible to describe, he unleashes the richest resources of his vocabulary in an attempt to do the job himself. The result is a colorful series of set-pieces and anecdotes.

There are accounts of Cobb's descending into the canyon on the back of a mule, of ex-cowboys and other colorful characters who are hired to create the local color of the "wild West" for visitors whose preconceived notions demand such catering, and of practical jokes like the tale of the "hydrophoby skunks" who supposedly fasten their teeth in the ears of tourists who are sleeping at night on the floor of the canyon. The account is a good example of Cobb's flair for creating a high order of travel literature out of his own intensely subjective experience.

In "How Do You Like the Climate?" Cobb turns his attention to Southern California. In the East, people have weather, he contends, but in Southern California there is no weather—only climate. "Its scenery looks as though it belonged on a stage—as though it should be painted on a curtain," he writes, though he warns the visitor to avoid wandering into this beautiful scenery "because out from under a rock will crawl a real estate agent" (118).

"In the Haunt of the Native Son" is an essay on San Francisco. The residents of this fabled bayside city, says Cobb, "do not strike you as being Westerners or as being transplanted Easterners; they are San Franciscans" (140). Moreover, he contends that the city retains a romantic aura, despite the claims of San Franciscans that all the romance is gone. He recommends the San Francisco restaurants over those of any other American city, but San Francisco's chief product, he says, is Native Sons.

"Looking for Lo," the last of the travel narratives in *Roughing It Deluxe,* is a whimsical essay on the Indians of the American West and Southwest. In all his travels through these portions of the United States Cobb saw only a few Indians, though he had expected to observe large numbers of them in their native dress. "If it is your desire to observe the Red Indian of the plains engaged in his tribal sports and pastimes," says Cobb, "wait for the Wild West Show" (175).

In this essay Cobb also describes his brief trip to Tijuana, Mexico, and to the Mormon capital at Salt Lake City. Most of the natives of Tijuana appeared to spend their time selling souvenirs to tourists, and in Salt Lake City Cobb was disappointed in his hopes of "seeing Indians on the hoof and Mormon households taking the air in family groups" (216).

In 1924, Cobb wrote and published six little travel volumes on various states of the United States. Ranging from fifty to a little over sixty pages, these compact books are primarily humorous essays, forming a set that Cobb labels "The American Guyed Book Series." In the book on Maine, he explains his purpose in writing the series. "The plan I have in mind," he says, "is to pick out certain states which appear to have personalities, individualities of their own, special and distinct characteristics in climate or politics or their social aspects or their scenic arrangements or their whatnot, and write little books about them" (11).

Two of the "Guyed Books" deal with Kentucky and North Carolina as representative of the border South and the South respectively. "Never could a Kentuckian be confused with a Middle Westerner," writes Cobb, "notwithstanding that merely the width of the Ohio River separates him from Ohio and Indiana and Illinois" (*K,* 28). Of North Carolina Cobb writes that she has everything but a press agent and that at the time of writing she is "the foremost State of the South in material progress, in public spirit, in educational expansion and in optimism of outlook" (*K,* 50).

Representing the Middle West are "Guyed Books" on Indiana and Kansas. Of Indiana Cobb writes that "she is the most typically American State in the American democracy" (14), and that she "holds by the pioneering culture and its offshoots—old-fashioned cookery, old-fashioned decencies, old-fashioned virtues, old-fashioned vices, old-fashioned bigotries, old-fashioned philosophies springing out of the soil and smelling of the pennyrile and the sassafrack" (49). The "Guyed Book" on Kansans consists largely of personal anecdotes, by means of which Cobb demonstrates the peculiar characteristics of Kansas, particularly the tendency of Kansans to act as the moral legislators of the whole country.

The other two "Guyed Books" are devoted to states in the East and Northeast—to New York and to Maine respectively. Cobb argues that the great New York metropolis is "the one densely inhabited locality—with the possible exception of Hell—that has absolutely not a trace of local pride" (29). Turning his attention to the famous Maine forestlands, he says, "You may go into the Maine woods all desk-sore and fagged and nervous, but the woods themselves will provide the tonic and the cure" (41). Besides the woods, however, the people of Maine are a very hardy breed whose ingenuity and stolidity must never be underestimated.

In 1926 Cobb added "Guyed Book" essays upon California, Wyoming, Texas, Wisconsin, Oregon (two essays), Virginia, New Jersey, Arizona, Louisiana, and Eastern Canada. By combining these essays with the six "America Guyed Book" essays, he created a substantial book which he published under the title *Some United States.*

By the time Cobb had published his essays and books on foreign and domestic travel, it was obvious to readers all over America, and to large numbers abroad, that Irvin Cobb was capable of seeing almost everything through the same pair of "funny glasses" that he had implicitly worn as the writer of humorous newspaper columns during his first few months on the *New York World.* Moreover, since he had established himself in the minds of his readers as "the funny fat man" on the one hand and as "the born loser" on the other, he was in a position to capitalize upon his public image for as long as his literary guises proved to be fruitful sources of humor.

In several important ways, however, Cobb was an astute self-critic, and he did not overestimate the potential of his various literary personae. Early in his career he had learned that the writing of humor is a fickle and perverse mistress who delights in causing one's best strokes to fall flat, while readers chuckle unaccountably over something the author has regarded as only moderately funny, if funny at all. As a result, Cobb armed himself with some self-imposed principles that helped to minimize these failures by appealing to the sympathy and good will of the reader. First, he avoided humorous thrusts that might conceivably alienate any individual among his readers. Second, and in a general way more important, he conveyed to his readers the impression that he was laughing at himself as willingly as he laughed at other people.

He was so thoroughly convinced of the need for this particular rapport between the reader and the writer of humor that he once publicly castigated some of his fellow humorists for "assuming, wittingly or unwittingly, an air of superiority . . . as though they sat on a high pinnacle in a rarified atmosphere of aloofness, looking down pityingly from that great height upon the foolish, futile, scrambling little human ants far beneath them, and stirring up those ants with barbed satire and clever ridicule." He concludes the passage with a practical pronouncement: "The man who aspires to be known as a humorist must constantly be saying, not, 'What fools *those* mortals be,' but 'What fools *all* mortals be—myself prominently included.'"[12]

Though humorous writers of later generations may not have consciously adopted and perpetuated this creed, Cobb can be said to have "set styles in humorous writing that still live. Many a youngster who never heard of Irvin S. Cobb, strives to emulate his style in writing a humor column for his high school paper."[13] This comment upon the influence of Cobb's humorous writing appeared as recently as the mid-1970s. In many respects this is one of the highest accolades a writer can hope to achieve—that of unconscious imitation.

Chapter Four
The Lonesome Laugh

Irvin Cobb did not achieve a nationwide reputation as a humorist until he had met and conquered the most blasé and sophisticated readers and audiences in America—the New Yorkers. But in New York his rise was amazingly swift. On 13 December 1901, he first appeared before a public gathering as a teller of humorous stories. The occasion was the annual dinner of the Thirteen Club, where he was introduced as "the Funnyglass Philosopher"—a tribute to the success of his early newspaper column "New York Through Funny Glasses." At first he suffered a severe case of stage fright. Nevertheless, he was an enormous success, and thereafter he was exhilarated by the challenge of public speaking. In less than two years he became one of America's most widely sought platform speakers, and almost to the end of his life he entertained audiences with his seemingly inexhaustible repertory of humorous anecdotes and oral stories.

Once Cobb had mastered the closely allied arts of oral humor and the humorous magazine article, his advent into the lucrative field of humorous fiction seems to have followed almost as a matter of course. Though at first the writing of fiction did not come easy to him, he was, as always, prepared to labor until the magazine and book publishers competed for his short stories as urgently as they had ever sought his articles.

In a broad and illuminating sense, Cobb's success as an after-dinner speaker and as a writer of humorous fiction and nonfiction has always been the most widely celebrated aspect of his career, even though he sometimes regretted the perversity of a public that failed to recognize his capacity to write equally well in other literary modes. For Cobb, the evocation of humor was always a desperate and painful business which he once characterized as "The Trail of the Lonesome Laugh."[1]

Topical and Occasional Humor

As a writer of topical and occasional humor, Irvin Cobb was almost constantly in the public eye. He had evolved quite naturally from a

writer of syndicated humorous columns in the newspapers to a writer
of topical humor for the national magazines. Throughout his career he
retained a foothold in both media, and his readers were used to seeing
his humorous comments upon matters of moment in both the newspapers and the magazines. In 1923, for instance, he was at home in
the *Literary Digest* with this comment upon the urgent question of
censorship: "The reason why we are threatened with censorship is because we have too much sensualship. I am against both. I believe in
free speech, but I don't believe in being free and easy."[2] But to the end
of his career his humorous commentary upon timely or merely commonplace concerns appeared also in the major newspapers, as for example these observations upon current politics in the 1930s: "The
average smart crook is a Republican and the average smart idiot is a
Democrat. Under ordinary conditions people at large, when it comes
to casting a vote, prefer smart crooks to honest damn fools."[3]

So widely known and appreciated were Cobb's droll observations
upon politics that during the political ferment of 1920 a magazine
writer suggested that "if Irvin Cobb had but been nominated, and
pledged to a daily statement upon the state of the nation and the feelings of a first-rate Presidential candidate, Warren Harding would not
even have been in the 'also ran' class."[4] Moreover, Cobb had interviewed and written about so many contemporary celebrities that other
interviewers found themselves wallowing in his wake, as did so eminent a man as Herbert Bayard Swope when Swope applied for an interview with Rudyard Kipling.[5]

Eventually, Cobb himself became a topic of current interest, and
almost to his last days the magazines sought his droll comments upon
his personal interests, even to the beginnings of his fatal illness, when
his multitudinous readers had been told prematurely that he was already dead. As he lay suffering, he wrote "a facetious letter making
jokes about doctors ('for a while they tried too hard to be cheerful, if
you know what I mean') and about the local undertaker ('his interest
was almost touching for a while')."[6] As one writer observed, "Mr.
Cobb's humor meets us at the cradle and follows us through all the
peripatetics of work, play, love, tailoring, haircutting, shaving and
manicuring."[7]

Irvin Cobb versus Mary Roberts Rinehart

"Oh! Well! You Know How Women Are!" (1920) is a clever stunt of
publication wherein the publishers brought together two of the best-

known writers of the time, Mary Roberts Rinehart and Irvin S. Cobb. The purpose of the literary prestidigitation was to engage these two celebrities in a contest to discover which writer could outdo the other in the eternal argument over the inferiority or superiority of the sexes. In this mock literary debate Rinehart, who had become famous as a writer of mystery thrillers when she published *The Circular Staircase* in 1908, refused to risk her delicacy as a well-bred woman or her popularity as an author by publicly ridiculing men in her essay called "Isn't That Just Like a Man?" Contending that women in general do not take themselves as seriously as men do, Rinehart pursued the theme that men are not really men at all. "There are grown-up boys, and middle-aged boys, and elderly boys, and sometimes very old boys," she argued. "But the essential difference is simply exterior. Your man is always a boy" (11).

Cobb's rejoinder, "Oh! Well! You Know How Women Are!" began as a narrative about the "typical" behavior of women as they went shopping, gossiped, rode street cars, and otherwise revealed the peculiarities of their sex. Though Cobb was sometimes more condescending toward women than Rinehart was toward men, he was often disarmingly liberal in his attitude toward the sex "of the opposite persuasion." He was not merely in favor of giving women the suffrage, for instance, but he welcomed them into the political arena as active participants. He closed with a high compliment to women, and with a surprising twist to the meaning of the titular phrase (32-33):

To the women fell the tasks which for the most part brought no public recognition, no public acknowledgments of gratitude. For them, instead of the palms of victory and the sheaves of glory, there were the crosses of sacrifice, the thorny diadems of suffering. We cannot conceive of men, thus circumstanced, going so far and doing so much. But the women—
  Oh, well, you know how women are!

Meanwhile, Cobb had considerable fun taking the conventional male "digs" at women. In doing so, he demonstrated that he had unsuspected skill in the phrasing of the witty epigram, which—at least in the opinions of most scholars and critics—constitutes the main distinction between the humor of Will Rogers and the humor of Irvin S. Cobb. When a woman meets an acquaintance, says Cobb, "If she likes the other woman, she is cordial. But if she does not like her she is very, very cordial" (7). That kind of witticism seems strongly reminiscent of the blasé and sophisticated humor of Oscar Wilde. Moreover, concerning women in politics, Cobb says, "Better the hand that rocks the cradle than the hand that rocks the boat" (15).

The two essays were brought together in one volume, with each piece bound upside down and backward, so that each essay begins inside one of the covers and ends in the middle of the book. This trick of bookbinding allows each cover "top billing" for either writer.[8] Irvin Cobb needed only the right occasion and an appropriate literary vehicle in order to demonstrate that he had a surprising flair for phrasing the witty maxim, partly in the mode of Oscar Wilde and partly in the "wise-crack" style of the Algonquin Wits.[9]

"Here Comes the Bride—"

Cobb's first substantial collection of his own topical and occasional humor is "Here Comes the Bride—" and So Forth (1925). The volume contains twenty-six essays in topical humor, of which the first is the titular essay.[10] Cobb argues that almost from her birth an American girl is in constant preparation for her wedding day. But chances are that modern marriages will not last. The reason, says Cobb, is that "Marriage used to be a contract; now so many seem to regard it as a ninety-day option" (19). Cobb closes with humorous anecdotes about the ridiculous paraphernalia of weddings, including typical wedding guests, especially distant relatives.

The next essay, "Some Crying Needs," is essentially a humorous editorial in which Cobb proposes reforms for a variety of commonplace annoyances. He advocates reforms in table manners, condemning in particular the "open-face feeder" (44) and people with long, drooping mustaches; and he roundly condemns the North American sleeping-car, with its bad ventilation, its windows that will not open, and its useless green hammocks. Because in this essay he has already branded the professional reformer a bore, Cobb follows through with "A Handy Pocket Guide to Bores." "A typical bore," says Cobb, "is a person who thinks if only he is sociable enough that he must also be popular. The bedbug makes the same mistake" (71). As crashing examples he cites Coleridge's Ancient Mariner and the various bores in Shakespeare's plays. Among other bores, Cobb mentions spiritualists, people who organize ship's concerts, and actors who insist upon reviving Shakespeare. Then Cobb halts abruptly for fear that he may be boring his readers.[11]

"The Funniest Thing That Ever Happened to Me" is an expanded anecdote drawn from Cobb's experiences as a correspondent in World War I. Turning from his war experiences to the proved and popular vein of "Cobb's Anatomy" and "Speaking of Operations—" he provides for this collection an equally entertaining piece called "But I Kept My Teeth." In "Open Season on Ancestors," Cobb looks forward—perhaps unwittingly—to the time when he will hire a battery of genealogists to uncover the roots of his family tree. From his humorous treatment of the perennially popular quest of ancestry, Cobb goes back into classical mythology with "that Piker Hercules." The main argument of this essay is that if Hercules had had to keep from going bald and to take off weight at the same time, he would not appear to be the great hero of mythology that he is.

"Who's Who at Our Zoo" compares Cobb's favorite domestic animals with those at the Bronx Zoo. Interspersed with such folktales as that of the hoop snake, the essay discusses unusual birds and exotic animals; and it closes with an anecdote about a traveling circus that advertised a "new-born" lion at every performance for six weeks. This reference to the general gullibility of the public introduces the next selection, "Trade," which deals with Cobb's gullibility to the arguments of expert salesmen. He has no resistance to the ploys of those agents who go from door to door selling books. "I am a natural-born buyer," he confesses, "but I am no seller" (211). As evidence, he says that in his youth he had failed miserably as an insurance agent. Had he succeeded, quips Cobb, "I might now be the kind of writer who makes a fortune by writing—I refer to the one who writes insurance" (217).

Turning again to one of his favorite topics, under the title of "Our National Holidays," Cobb offers some variations upon the reliable quips with which he used to introduce the annual holidays in his newspaper columns. "A Noble Industry Declines" is an outgrowth of Cobb's reportorial attendance at hundreds of court trials, and the "noble industry" of which he speaks is that of the expert insanity witness. Cobb declares that "the gentle art of expert witnessing" (253) reached its peak at a time when the statutes were unclear concerning the difference between medical insanity and legal insanity. But in a recent case when a "fireworky financier" hired thirteen alienists to prove that he was insane, the jury found him sane. Now, says Cobb, "the business of expert insanity testifying has gone into a decline" (259).

As one of the most widely sought after-dinner speakers in the country, Cobb wields the authority of experience when he writes "The Mod-

ern Tommy Tuckers," as he also does later in "Unaccustomed as I
Am—."[12] Comparing the modern after-dinner speaker with the legendary Tommy Tucker who sang for his supper, Cobb estimates that
between March and October there are at least fifty dinners in New York
every night. Moreover, all of the diners are fated to be regaled by one
of the typical after-dinner speakers—"Congressman Coma and General
Stupor and Major Laffan Gass the noted wit, and Professor Morphine
and Doctor Opiate, each with a speech in his system and a firm intention of working it off before it begins to mold on him" (266). Obviously drawing upon recollections of his first after-dinner speech, Cobb
describes the tortures the neophyte after-dinner speaker must suffer.
But in spite of these awful tortures, Cobb marvels, "the seeds of the
deadly after-dinner speaking habit have been instilled into his nature,
and he is a lost soul from that hour henceforward" (271).

Deciding that it might be a form of public service to argue the
benefits of being "homely with a stalwart and sterling homeliness
which is neither to be gainsaid nor denied" (277), Cobb wrote "The
Advantage of Being Homely," which he reprinted in this collection.
From earliest childhood, says Cobb, the handsome man is spoiled by
indiscriminate attentions, while homely men, "unvexed by miscellaneous kissing in their babyhood, by curls and black plush panties in
their boyhood, by mash notes in their adolescence, and by mirror-
worship in their manhood, are leading the world's armies and shaping
the world's commerce" (279).

Then, harking back to the time when he was commuting between
his country home and his city work, Cobb appeared to realize that he
still had not told everything about that period of his life. Accordingly,
he wrote "Our German Garden," which was really only a small flower
bed. Ignorant of the rudiments of the enterprise, Cobb had hired an
expert German gardener who, after a number of comic disasters, has
to be fired. But within a few days tiny bugs appear, and the plants
begin to look "like Irish lace" (301). All that survives is a volunteer
onion that has sprung up among the flowers.

Following "The Gold Brick Twins," a piece of humorous fiction that
is out of place in the collection of essays, Cobb concludes the volume
with an occasional piece called "Christmas Gifts." Creating his own
version of the Adam and Eve story as an analogue, Cobb argues that at
Christmas the usual gift-giving arrangement is archetypal. For the husband, says Cobb, the true Christmas spirit lies in his feeling that he
must give his wife "the things she wants most and having her give you
the things she wants next to most" (330).

Prose and Cons

In *Prose and Cons* (1926), Cobb includes four pieces of topical humor to fill out a miscellaneous collection of humorous fiction. "Long Pants," which was first published as "The Long Pants Age" in the August 1925 issue of *Good Housekeeping,* could serve as a companion piece to the "Little Short Pantsleroy" chapter of *Goin' on Fourteen.* In Cobb's memories of his boyhood, the long pants phase succeeds the childhood phase that is characterized by "knee britches." The key to this essay is Cobb's memory of that moment when his first pair of full-length trousers represents his passage from boyhood to manhood. Hoping also for a pair of splendiferous shirt-cuffs like those of his sartorial hero the drugstore clerk, he is considerably deflated to receive only plain suspenders and gray jeans. Even so, he is deceived into feeling that he is now a man, and for the first time he takes a girl to the circus, where in a most juvenile way he creates a riot by way of a practical joke.

This episode is succeeded by another childhood reminiscence, "The Thrill of a Life-Time,"[13] a variation in viewpoint upon an incident he has told before. Here, in a childhood escapade comparable with those in Mark Twain's *Tom Sawyer,* young Cobb and three other teenage boys tie an old coffee pot to the tail of a stray dog. "I don't suppose any dog ever succeeded in running entirely out of his own skin," Cobb says of such dogs, "but . . . they always appeared to be trying hard to do it" (281). Seeing that the dog and the elaborate funeral cortege of a deceased local veterinarian are about to have a confrontation on a very narrow bridge, Cobb and another boy hide in a culvert beneath. In the transcendent confusion that ensues, the rearing horses throw the coffin into the culvert. As the coffin stands on end, the lid opens, and the corpse of Old Doc Wheeler stands facing the two boys as though accusing the culprits. "Fully ten years elapsed before I quit dreaming dreams of a grievously interrupted funeral," says Cobb, "and I was nearing my thirtieth birthday before I began to see any humor in the event" (292–93). This is one of Cobb's most durable anecdotes.

"Unaccustomed As I Am—" provides Cobb with a long-sought opportunity to explain the bizarre circumstances that launched him on his career as an after-dinner speaker. Buttonholing Cobb one afternoon, a theatrical agent convinced him to sign a contract to lecture about the war. Following the agent's suggestion that he learn all he can from the "travelhog boys," (264) Cobb attends a travelogue and is dismayed by the splendid appearance and the poise of the speaker. Then he buys a book on elocution, but mostly it contains drawings of a man in postures expressing the major emotions. Recognizing this elocutionary system as that of Delsarte, he firmly resolves "to be sartorially correct without being Delsartorial" (267). To his surprise he is a success. The paid performer, he concludes, always has the sympathy of the audience, even over local hecklers. The reason is that Americans have great "tolerance for the under dog so long as the under dog shows an inclination to bite back" (278).

The last humorous essay in *Prose and Cons* is "Shakspere's Seven Ages and Mine." Here Cobb translates Shakespeare's definitions of the "seven ages of man" into modern terms and discovers droll differences between sixteenth-century attitudes and those of the twentieth. Today, he argues, instead of an infant "muling and puking in his mother's arms" a child is born "according to estimates and reared by plans and specifications" (295). He agrees with Shakespeare's picture of the schoolboy, but he chastizes the bard for skipping the period of adolescent "calf-love" to get to the age of the mature lover. Moreover, he argues that the age of the soldier no longer exists but that justices still have the "fair round belly." Of one's present-day station in life after the age of fifty he remarks that a man is "either a headpin or a pinhead. If you are a pinhead nobody takes you seriously, and if you are a headpin you are stood up as a target and the world bowls at you" (351).

The Folks at Home

Along with the ten travel essays in *Both Sides of the Street* (1930) Cobb includes four loosely grouped essays in topical humor under the heading of "The Folks Here at Home."[14] The first of these, "Golfitis; Its Curse and Cure," is primarily a good-natured criticism of the planning of golf courses. This whimsical discussion gives way to "Is There a Second to the Motion?" which is also a humorous complaint against so-called "improvements." The first part of the essay is a lament for the loss of healthful attitudes among people. "Why is it that so many of the younger intelligentsia seem to have so much trouble deciding which sex they're going to belong to, if either?" he inquires. In the next paragraph he demands to know "Why is it now good breeding to appear ill-bred?" (262).

"Wall Street's Leap Year" is a humorous essay upon the politics of that day, though it is also a lament for the passing of the rabid political campaigns of the 1920s. "When it comes to being nervous," he says, "Wall Street is a rabbit's nose" (281). During every presidential campaign, therefore, Wall Street goes "jumping crazy."

The last essay in this group, "Life on the Bounding Red Ink," is an exercise in the mock epic. Cobb opens the essay with a mock-epic version of the classical invocation: "Hearken whilst I sing of the amateur yachtsman." Developing the essay through a mock-epic catalog, he lists in three groups those people who have this particular "mental disease"—the man who has just acquired a tiny motor-boat or a skiff; the man who was born with the disease and who has a medium sized yacht; and the wealthy man who maintains "a large slick yacht complete with tradesmen's entrances and hot and cold running stewards" (299). Returning sporadically to mock epic diction,[15] Cobb has great fun in tracing the various stages of the yachtsman's disease from his purchase of an old motor boat through the second, third, and fourth vessels according to the owner's improving station in life. The yachtsman is nearly bankrupt before he fully realizes that "nothing that's second-handed loses value so rapidly as a yacht, unless it's false teeth" (307).

It is not surprising that the American people now remember Irvin Cobb as a humorist. Though he was one of the most versatile writers of his time, his vast exposure as a humorist has understandably eclipsed his earlier reputation as a local colorist, as a creator of horror and mystery tales, and as a tireless writer of miscellaneous fiction in which he has employed most of the common American dialects. From the time when his fellow newsmen on the *Sun* began to leave the city room to hear Cobb tell his stories in the hallway, his reputation as a raconteur spread rapidly across the country. Every day he printed a funny story in the columns of his own newspaper. Soon the stories were syndicated, and people all over the nation could read them in their local newspaper.

Two Treasuries of Funny Stories

By 1923 he had collected his syndicated stories, one for every day of the year and a "Special Extra—to Be Read Only in Leap Year"— under the title of *A Laugh a Day Keeps the Doctor Away*. In the foreword he argues that Americans, more than any other people, have made the humorous anecdote "a part of our daily life, using it to point morals, to express situations, to help us solve puzzles." He chose for his collection those stories he personally liked best, and it is a monument to his taste that he selected only one mother-in-law story and not a single story in which "a colored character is referred to as 'Rastus.'"

In 1925, Cobb produced a similar collection titled *Many Laughs for Many Days*. Of all Cobb's books, his two collections of humorous anecdotes appear to have enjoyed the greatest longevity. To the present day—largely because members of civic groups regard them as rich sources of material for after-dinner speeches—these two books remain in almost constant circulation from the public libraries.[16]

Sad-Faced Humor and the Classic Quip

Much of Cobb's reputation as an entertaining after-dinner speaker and a master of the humorous anecdote is due to the tenacity with which large numbers of people respond to the "funny story." By now it seems clear that Irvin Cobb "greatly entertained his generation"[17] and that by publishing most of his material in book form he became more than "a newspaper humorist, maker of the most volatile of all literary products."[18] Because truly competent humorists are rare in literary history, moreover, they sometimes survive by virtue of their rarity. For this reason their humorous writings frequently outlast other works of equal or superior literary value. "A man may write serious fiction for ten years and do straight reportorial work for ten years," says Cobb, "but let him turn out one piece of foolery that tickles the public in the short ribs and, from that hour, he is branded as a humorist."[19] The tone of this remark casts some doubt upon assumptions that Cobb wished to be remembered primarily as a humorist or that he has "won and held his place in literature by advocating the cause of laughter."[20]

Cobb's reputation as a humorist has survived because, like all true humorists, Cobb was more than a mere clown or jokester. He was keenly aware of this difference, as he indicates when he says, "Humor for the sake of the laugh, like the cartoon born for the sake of the popular mood, has no lasting value."[21] Like the humor of Mark Twain, that of Cobb tends to arise from serious matters, and in the sidelong fashion that is typical of effective humor, it makes a meaningful commentary. For this reason primarily, Cobb has been most often compared with Twain.[22] Indeed, one can say as truthfully of Cobb as of Twain that "the striking thing about a genuine humorist is that he knows with precision when to be in earnest."[23]

Cobb was at bottom a serious-minded man who found that he could often make the most effective commentaries through the use of humor. When as a small child "Buff" Cobb was told that her father was a person who wrote funny things to make people laugh, she said, "That can't be my Daddy. . . . He's never bery entertaining around the house."[24] In the candor of childhood, she had expressed what most people seem to believe—that humorists are effortlessly funny all the time. Like most people who have never really thought about the matter, she did not realize "that humorists are not paid to be funny at home."[25] Indeed, as Cobb demonstrates by means of a mock-serious self-portrait he inserted into "The Trail of the Lonesome Laugh," the writing of genuine humor is usually the product of conscious effort and hard labor:

when he sits down at his typewriter and slips a clean, unsullied sheet of paper into the machine, his associates [fellow newspaper reporters] glance inquiringly at him; and if a look of intense pain comes over his face; and if his brows knit together in deep corrugations, and his gills begin to pant up and down with slow, convulsive movements, and he emits low, groaning sounds, then those who cannot bear the sight of suffering arise and tiptoe off, saying to one another as they go:

"Come, let us go away from here. Our poor friend is getting ready to write something funny."[26]

Much of Cobb's success in the precarious fields of topical humor and oral anecdote can be attributed to his wide interests and his capacity for discriminating between the funny and the unfunny. "Cobb is a great humorist," observes Grant Overton, "because he is most other things first."[27] Cobb shares with other genuine humorists a rare capacity to endow the comic with philosophic overtones that arise from his depth and complexity as a human being. In this regard, few American humorists have more deserved the accolade an English scholar and essayist has conferred upon Cobb: "Beneath Mr. Cobb's fun is a mass of ripe experience and sagacity. However playful he may be on the surface, one is aware of an almost Johnsonian universality beneath. It would not be extravagant to call his humor the bloom on the fruit of the tree of knowledge."[28]

Moreover, Cobb had a keen perception of the necessary relationship between the writer and the reader of humorous essays. Sometimes, in order to clarify this relationship, he takes the reader directly into his confidence, as he does early in one humorous essay upon an essentially serious topic. "Should this minstral bard strive at ill-advised moments

to interject a lighter tone into the motif," he says, "that merely will
be because he is the kind who probably would snicker if something
funny happened during a funeral and has been known to laugh right
out at interpretive dancing."[29]

In the oral rendition of humorous anecdotes, Cobb was a purist.
Always, whether he was telling a story to an acquaintance at lunch or
addressing a large crowd in an auditorium, his delivery was remarkable
for careful selection of detail, for the measuring of emphasis and proportion, for the judicious management of suspense, for effective timing, and for the active and lively use of dialect. Above all, Cobb refused
to violate the language for the sake of colloquial effects. Looking back
upon her life, his daughter "Buff" recalls that "he told stories, funny
ones, dramatic ones, and sad ones, better than anyone else in the
world. First place he was a great mimic. . . . Why I've seen that man
look more like a lobster than a lobster does. . . . Also his speech was
more colorful, more vivid and saltier than his writing. He always had
the unexpected, the fantastic word at his tongue's end, and he was one
of the few people I ever knew who, in this degenerate age, spoke in
complete sentences. He never chopped off a phrase or forgot a verb or
a predicate. This gave even an improvisation the finish of a conscious
work."[30] Indeed, all the evidence indicates that Cobb had disciplined
himself as severely in the craft of oral storytelling as in the craft of
written composition.

Despite his native gifts as a teller of oral anecdotes and tales, Cobb
had to train himself rigorously in some aspects of his calling. Though
a large, listening crowd seemed to him at first a fearful thing, the
instantaneous responses of a gathering forced him to marshall unknown
resources. His daughter noticed that "audiences became of increasing
importance to him. They brought him to life, or gave it an accentua-
tion and clarity that was lost to him without their aid."[31]

But because unresponsive or recalcitrant audiences distressed him,
he had to learn painfully and through long experience that a speaker
must cultivate the right attitudes toward an audience. He had to learn,
for instance, that no matter how well a speaker might perform, the
man who seeks to entertain a large group "must be sure of one thing.
He must like his audience. If he comes before them out of a dripping
rain, gruff and unhappy in mood, he had better stop in the wings and
shake off that mood or he will convey his feelings to the crowd and
they will not like him."[32]

Throughout his life, Irvin Cobb spontaneously looked upon much of the world in the spirit of comedy. Like all genuine humorists, he habitually "thought funny," which is not to say, though, that his humor was always benign. Sometimes it was bitter or ironic, as when he first heard that his notoriously tough and generally feared *World* editor, "Hard-boiled Charlie" Chapin, was ill. "Let's hope it's nothing trivial,"[33] said Cobb. And sometimes his remarks were puckish or wry, as when editor Thomas B. Costain asked him to respond to a questionnaire containing the item "First efforts in writing, and success, if any." Cobb wrote in the blank, "Newspaper work at 17 as reporter; I succeeded, the paper failed."[34] Whenever asked of his religion, he usually replied that he was "just an innocent bystander."[35] These are but quips, of course, but they were so widely known, quoted, and appreciated that one commentator said of them, "His quips became classic."[36]

Short Fiction: Sweat as Punctuation

When Irvin Cobb first entertained the idea of writing short fiction, his decision fostered in him a degree of apprehension that is difficult to reconcile with the success which for years he had enjoyed as one who could relate successfully a wide variety of essays, articles, anecdotes, and oral stories. But so high a regard did he have for all categories of his craft that he never underestimated the demands of writing in any form. Having learned from experience that the process of composing a really good article or essay is like condemning oneself to a term in prison, he was now convinced that writing a good short story would be a term at hard labor in the quarries of the imagination.

"Every smooth, easy, graceful line," Cobb declares, "means another furrow in the forehead of its maker. Nearly every recorded statement which deals with the verities means study, research, and patient inquiry."[37] To such a writer as Cobb, who said without insincere modesty that on the ladder to the top of his profession he was still "clutching at the lowermost rounds,"[38] there seemed little reason to be confident in beginning to practice a literary form he had never regarded as his domain.

Because Cobb had always considered grueling effort one of the facts of his calling, he despised the legions of would-be authors who merely "dash off" this or that literary composition. Of this attitude he says, "You should see me some morning when I'm in the mood for dashing off the stuff. There I sit, dashing it off at the rate of about an inch and a half an hour, and using drops of sweat for punctuation. I am the same

sort of impetuous dasher the Muir Glacier is. And so is every writer I
know who is getting by with it."[39] There are many examples of the
lengths to which he went in order to verify his details, but the most
illuminating one is his preparation for a short story called "The Unbroken Chain." Near the end of the narrative, his main character cries
out two words in the dialect of a small African tribe. By the time Cobb
was ready to write the two words, he explains, "they represented the
total results of three full days which I had spent at the New York
Public Library, going through books on African tribes . . . , and also
going through two enormous dictionaries of the tongues of African
tribes, with the English translations."[40]

Cobb's preparatory strategies for writing his first piece of short fiction were even more elaborate and painstaking. The story is "The Escape of Mr. Trimm," and it is the first of his highly successful tales of
the eerie and the bizarre. From the vantage afforded by nearly half a
century, one can only marvel that Cobb's preparations for writing did
not utterly ruin the story by a species of overkill. Moreover, contrary
to the practice of the large numbers of professional writers who fear
that they will "talk away" their current stories,[41] Cobb sought out close
friends like Bozeman Bulger, with whom he explored almost endlessly
his ideas for the story.[42] This kind of thoroughness carried over into
the writing of all Cobb's fiction, however light or farcical some of it
came to be.

Humorous Fiction: Farce, Gimmickry, Irony

By 1911, Cobb was aware that the times were unmistakably moving
toward a preference for fictional humor over the humorous essay. In a
letter to an acquaintance in St. Louis, he wrote, "If I were going to
talk on your subject, I should take the attitude that the recent tendencies in American Humor—if any such there be?—are toward the clothing of humor in the form of fiction, as witness Harry Leon Wilson, O.
Henry, and Tarkington for conspicuous example—in other words that
we are tending toward the Dickens vehicle rather than toward the Bill
Nye school of pure burlesque."[43]

Cobb was convinced that the nature of humor is essentially the same
for fiction as for the humorous anecdote and essay. The only important
difference is that the writer of fiction must be able to use a different
medium for achieving humorous effects, and after Cobb had written
his first few humorous stories, he decided that the short story was, if

anything, superior to the topical or the occasional essay as a vehicle for humor. For one thing, he discovered that the short story tends to be far more universal in its appeal. "One man's humor is another man's poison," he wrote in the introduction to his own collection of the best humorous stories. "Nothing is so ephemeral as topical humor. Nothing so soon gets antiquated as humor unless it be an egg or a war movie."[44]

But when humor is cast in the form of fiction, he decided, it has one important advantage over other forms of humorous writing. In fiction, humor tends to arise directly from the concerns of the characters who are essential to the narrative. And these concerns lie deep in the unchanging nature of human beings: "Somebody said once that man was the only creature who laughs. A happy dog grins and a pleased horse shows his teeth and a parrot cackles in derisive mimicry of us. . . . Yet none of these actually laughs. But the man who mentioned this unique trait of our breeding didn't go far enough. He should have stated that while man alone laughs, he laughs his loudest and heartiest at the embarrassment and the undoing and the physical and mental torments of his own kind."[45] Indeed, says Cobb, coming up with his own definition of humor, "In the final summary I'd say humor, reduced to its basic principles, is tragedy standing on its head with its pants torn."[46]

From 1911 to the end of his career, Cobb by no means forsook the composition of topical and occasional humor, but he devoted increasing efforts to the writing of fiction, much of which was humorous. In adapting his talents to this kind of writing, however, he found that certain varieties of humor worked better in nonfiction than in the kinds of stories he wanted to write. Altogether he wrote a large number of farcical essays and articles, but he wrote only a few farcical short stories.[47]

One of Cobb's most obvious attempts at fictional farce is a long short story that was published as an illustrated booklet titled *The Life of the Party*.[48] Drawing upon the kind of broad humor he had already used frequently in essays and articles concerning preposterous fads in clothing, he created the character of Algernon Leary, a respectable if naive and prosaic New York attorney, who dressed in pink rompers for a fashionable costume party, going as "himself at the age of three." Surprised at his uncharacteristic ingenuity in rejecting the prevailing guise of little Lord Fauntleroy or Buster Brown, Leary basks in his hostess' assurances that he is "the life of the party."

But the moment he leaves the party he is beset by disasters. He is abandoned by a drunken taxi driver in a dark and sinister part of the city. A street-thief steals his overcoat, along with his wallet, card case, and latchkey. Now, dressed in his pocketless pink-satin rompers that are fastened by a row of big pearly buttons down the back, and supporting white stockings, pink garters, and patent leather slippers, Leary seeks help from members of a "pleasure club." But they laugh at him and bedevil him in the street. At length a police officer tries to disperse the crowd. Hoping to be jailed, Leary gives the policeman a violent shove. Instead of going straight to a cell, Leary gets the "bum's rush" toward a night court whose magistrate turns out to be his vicious rival in love. But with great luck, Leary escapes. Later, finding himself near the bachelor quarters of his law partner, he squeezes through the transom. His partner eventually gets home to find the pink-rompered Leary exhausted and almost unconscious. To Stark's demand to know what in heaven's name is going on, Leary responds, with a wan smile, "I've been the life of the party."

This story is typical of the farcical tour de force that Cobb was capable of writing, and most of these excursions into the broadly ridiculous found considerable if sometimes short-lived favor with the public. His talent for the farcical story begot a wide range of characters and situations. One story, "A Bull Called Emily,"[49] is an expanded anecdote and tall tale about a huge circus elephant in a private side show. The animal acquires such a fondness for peanuts that during a visit by school children it founders itself, runs amok, and devastates every peanut stand and vendor's cart in town.

In another farcical story, "The Gold Brick Twins,"[50] a perversion of Æsop's fable of the grasshopper and the ant serves as an exemplum for a tale of two shady characters who conspire with a lobbyist to defraud and blackmail a culpable legislator. Every character in the story turns out to be a crook. An example of Cobb's extraordinary range in farcical fiction is "The Order of the Bath."[51] As an exaggerated form of the once-popular American-versus-effete-Englishman motif, Cobb's story presents an impossibly snobbish English bore in the character of Jeffreys Boyce-Upchurch, a celebrated English novelist. Demanding to take baths in his own room but being refused by a host family whose house has only one bathroom, he gets his own way by climbing naked onto the roof in a rainstorm at night. But he steps on the soap, lands in a manure pile, has to cover himself with women's bloomers from a clothes line, and in this state appears before the whole family. His immediate departure for England leaves behind a relieved and amused family that has had its fill of English celebrities.

Many of Cobb's humorous stories depend upon and revolve around a gimmick created for the sole purpose of making the story "work." In the hands of an inept writer, this device seems a cheap trick and does not satisfy. But Cobb sometimes makes it work surprisingly well. Among Cobb's best and most obvious as well as successful gimmicks is the one he uses in "Red Handed."[52] After elaborate preparations, a clever thief has identified an ordinary parcel as containing a quarter of a million dollars in tightly rolled bills. Though the reader has not the least hint of the fact, the amount of money is the gimmick, and in keeping the gimmick concealed, Cobb never for an instant tips his hand.

The thief, Solitaire by name, contrives to waylay a disguised courier, take the money, hide it in the swamp, get himself thrown in jail for a few weeks on a minor offense, and go back afterward to get the money. All goes well, except that the minor offense he commits takes him before a tough judge who sentences him to hard labor for three months. Otherwise he is almost smug about his own cleverness. At the time of the robbery, he made sure he had the right courier by jabbing a gun into his ribs and demanding to know the contents of the package. Surprised and badly frightened, the man stuttered what sounded like "a q-q-quarter-of-a-million." That was Solitaire's man all right. And Solitaire had hidden the package well. So after suffering tortures through the months on a rock pile, Solitaire has the package in his trembling hands. He can hardly wait to get the "feel" of that quarter of a million dollars. The loot seems to be in a small can which, in unbearable anticipation, he opens—to find only red paint in a can boldly labeled "A Quart of Vermilion."

This gimmick is most precarious, depending as it does upon egregious coincidence and the necessity for the usual pronunciation of a common phrase to sound like something else when spoken under great stress. But Cobb makes the story work by justifying the coincidence and by successfully delaying disclosure until the very last words of the story. Though almost any reader senses that Cobb has put up a job on him, the author's clever manipulation of story line is likely to arouse more admiration than outrage.

But other stories that are dominated by gimmickry do not work as well. It is sometimes difficult to understand how Cobb's contemporary reputation remained so high while he perpetrated upon his public such tales as "Thank God for Modern Hotels,"[53] and "Nobody Sees the Waiter's Face."[54] In the former story a young woman runs nearly distracted to the door of another hotel guest whose typewriter has been clacking incessantly—to find that the man is a popular literary figure upon whom she has had a worshipful "crush." The other story is only an expanded exemplum based upon the adage that "nobody ever sees a waiter's face." Cobb liked to create gimmicks for his stories, and he built a large number of stories around them. Generally speaking, he succeeded better than might be expected with one of the most slippery devices in fiction writing.

Though most of Cobb's gimmicky stories have in them a perceptible irony, those that lead to a strongly ironic conclusion are frequently the best of their kind. In these stories, the strong ironies tend to provide better justification for the use of gimmicks. Sometimes a good story has in it together the elements of farce, gimmickry, and strong irony— elements that are not always compatible with each other.

One of the best examples of Cobb's use of this mixture is "How to Stop a Panic,"[55] which is built upon a clever and highly functional gimmick that Cobb derived from his knowledge of common banking practices of the time. The central character, one "Judge" 'Lonzo Steers, is a penurious and overcautious old man whose whole fortune amounts in round numbers to $2,500. As a hedge against imaginary bank failures, he has made a habit of transferring the money periodically from his account to a safety deposit box. But during a real crisis the town's bankers agree to refuse all extraordinary movements of money, and 'Lonzo's banker denies his request for the usual transfer.

So 'Lonzo starts walking from bank to bank with his money and is refused at each bank. He soon collects a large following of townspeople who find the spectacle amusing, and the parade takes on the character of a holiday in the town. But the boisterous mood of the crowd makes 'Lonzo fearful that somebody might snatch his bag of money from him. In a moment of inspiration, he hurries into the post office and puts the money into postal savings. The crowd, however, continues to find his predicament humorous. Especially, to his profound mortification, they all see a postal clerk entering his old bank to deposit 'Lonzo's money there—where it was in the first place. The whole crowd collapses in laughter in front of the bank.

Watching the spectacle with great relief, 'Lonzo's old banker tells his colleagues that the crisis is over. They no longer need fear a massive "run" on the bank because, as he says, "You get a whole community laughing at itself and it'll forget to be scared." So despite his purely selfish motives, 'Lonzo has saved the town from panic and financial disaster. The story is really a triumph of narrative irony, and in troubled financial times anywhere it has a perennial relevance.

For a writer best known for lighthearted jest and anecdote, Cobb was more often at his best in that dark and bitter form of humor that arises from ironies. One of his most widely read stories, "The Thunders of Silence,"[56] is a good example in point. Everything in this story stems from a potentially catastrophic anomaly in the American way of life— that of the megalomaniac obstructionist whom the public press creates and nurtures through its very efforts to destroy him. In Congressman Jason Mallard, Cobb creates the ultimate character of this type.

Endowed with superior powers of persuasion and peerless instincts for duplicity, Congressman Mallard always casts the only negative vote against every bill that is necessary to the perpetuation of the government and the survival of the country in time of war. By these and similar actions he has made himself a more dangerous enemy inside the country than our declared foreign enemies could ever be. His single vote, of course, is not in itself the danger. The real danger comes afterward, when, through puffed-up publicity in the newspapers, his voice in opposition reaches the ears of almost every literate citizen. As Quinlan, a washed-out but once-great newsman, says to a young reporter, "The under dog may be ever so bad a dog, but only let enough of us start kicking him all together, and what's the result? Sympathy for him—that's what."[57]

Quinlan's remedy is stunningly simple. The public press has made this cancer in the body politic, and by the same token, if it will, the press can destroy him. Since in every newspaper and periodical the constant thunder of his voice has become Jason Mallard's life blood, let all news media combine to give him hereafter only the thunders of silence. Because the time is right, cooperation is unanimous, and slowly, month by month Jason Mallard becomes a nonentity. Even his name is not mentioned, anywhere, by anybody, and in the end the thunders of silence become a force that drives him mad. In an obscure town in the midwest he throws himself into an ice-laden river and is gone completely and forever, as though he has never lived.

To Americans, this story has a disturbing timelessness. Since we have never known a time when the United States has been entirely safe from some real-life Jason Mallard, few Americans can read the story without a twinge of fear. The more complex grow the various media of modern communications and their systems, moreover, the less likely it seems that any such voluntary muzzling of the media can be possible.

Though in structure his short fiction is considered "dated," Cobb wrote some stories that appear surprisingly modern. More surprising yet, some of them deal with social issues that have become critical only in the later decades of the twentieth century. "This Man's World" (*TM*, 1–28), for instance, begins with a short treatise that could serve as a current argument on behalf of the Equal Rights Amendment. And the story that follows the treatise could be used as a case-study of pre-ERA attitudes toward the role of women in a society dominated by men.

At twenty-three and twenty-one respectively, Annie and Anita Crupper are sisters who work in a department store, making only a fraction of the salary of men and young boys at the same jobs. Eventually Annie marries a proud if middle-class steamfitter named Joe. At about the same time Anita goes to "live with" a shady but elegant character named Fred. "As a working man's wife," says Cobb the narrator, "the senior Miss Crupper would be respected but must pay for the respect with drudgery . . . , while the junior would go her sinful ways branded with the delectable and beautiful stigmata of the kept woman"(*TM*, 5–6).

Both men warn the sisters to stay away from each other. But despite these warnings, Anita, who is showered with luxuries and has time on her hands, begins in secret to give her fashionable and expensive cast-off clothes and jewelry to Annie, who is dowdy and burdened with housework. After a time, Annie begins accepting her sister's invitations to put on the beautiful cast-off things and go places with her during the day. But a scandalized neighbor of Annie's writes an anonymous note to Joe. When he finds that his "orders" have been disobeyed, he searches the house, finds the gifts from a "kept woman," and beats Annie. Painfully hurt and disheveled, she leaves the house and goes to Anita's—to find that Anita's consort has ordered her away because she is developing an unsightly goiter. The story ends with the sisters making new plans for the future while Anita says to Annie, "You go straight and I go crooked and the best either of us gets is the worst of it. Sis, what the hell's wrong with this rotten world, anyway?" For the reader, the question is purely rhetorical, since the title of the story is the answer—it's a man's world.

In this story, as in many of a similar kind, Cobb pushes humor to the edge of a narrow line that divides the comic from the serious. Many admirers of Cobb's fiction, then as now, have failed to recognize this kind of story as part of the author's legacy to American humor. The reason is that, in America, only the sophisticated reader has achieved the old-world perspective that allows him to perceive bitter ironies as a form of humor. As Vardis Fisher has argued, American humor remains essentially a frontier humor. The result is that American readers in general tend to distrust any humor that fails to elicit an urge to open laughter or to provide "a gentle ministering to our self esteem." Because our cultural history has been too short to acquire the *tonus* that comes only from long epochs of flux and vicissitude, we have not yet learned to recognize humor as at bottom "a defense against life and an admission of partial defeat."[58]

In "This Man's World," Cobb creates that seeming anomaly "serious humor." It is a story, like many similar ones by Cobb, in which "fate" or merely "life" behaves like some cosmic practical joker that enjoys perpetrating a cruel trick upon Annie and Anita. But it is nonetheless a joke and therefore a legitimate form of humor.

Humor and Humanity

One of the signal aspects of Cobb's career as humorist is that the nature of his humor underwent a radical change from the specific to the universal. Though the "funny stuff" of his early humor was frequently directed at current events and public personalities, he turned his mature humor inward upon himself as a representative of the ludicrous in the human condition. As he ripened as a humorist Cobb came fully to understand lessons he had learned from Mark Twain, whose influence he has frequently acknowledged. "I made Twain my model," he says, "and I studied his method. I came to the conclusion that what Mark was saying to mankind as a humorist was this, 'Look what fools we are, and I at the head of the procession.'"[59]

In the legacy of American humor, this quality saves Cobb from total obscurity and aligns him with standard American humorists like Bill Nye, Will Rogers, and Twain himself. In this regard, the estimate of an eminent American scholar and critic, William Rose Benét, was that "a selection from Cobb's work would make a book of characteristically American humor, to last for a long time. He stands somewhere between Mark Twain and Joel Chandler Harris in the American pantheon."[60]

The largeness, the inclusiveness—and the consequent avoidance of concern with soon-forgotten people and events—are qualities that help distinguish everyday journalistic humor from the kind that makes a place for itself in a literary heritage. They are also qualities that do not encourage the venting of personal bitterness for its own sake. And so it is with the fully developed humorous writing of Irvin Cobb. After an interview with Cobb, one writer was convinced that he "has a heart like a meeting-house . . . and thinks of humor as a triumph of good nature."[61] Whether he is a bemused narrator as in *The Life of the Party* or whether he is himself the genial subject of a piece as in *Speaking of Operations—*, he is always implicitly or explicitly a participator.

By virtue of his ability to include himself among the foolish, misguided, and often bumbling members of the human race, Cobb reached what is possibly the ultimate achievement of the significant humorist—a deep and tolerant understanding of the human condition. Knowing that "the first essential in a humorist is that he be a humanist,"[62] Cobb managed to do more with the blending of the humorous and the serious than have some of the best known humorous writers in American literature.

"The extraordinary thing about Cobb," observed Grant Overton, "is that he can turn a burst of laughter into a funeral oration, a snicker into a shudder and a smile into a crime. He writes in octaves, striking instinctively all the chords of humor, pathos, and romance with either hand."[63] This wide range and mix of emotion is especially effective in Cobb's short fiction, as Will Rogers acknowledged when he refused John Wilson Townsend's otherwise tempting invitation for Rogers to follow Cobb in transcribing into print the Charley Russell story that each considered Russell's best. "I can't write anything in a book following Irvin Cobb," replied Rogers. "Why that old Rascal can take the 10 Commandments and make 'em funny."[64]

In the closing decades of the twentieth century it is difficult to perceive the full extent of Cobb's popularity as a humorist during the 1920s and 1930s. A small incident, possibly apocryphal, was widely recounted at that time, and it goes far to suggest something about Cobb's influence upon the reading habits of the public. As the story goes, George Horace Lorimer, editor of the *Saturday Evening Post,* asked a newsdealer how the *Post* was selling that week. "They ask me whether there is anything in it by Cobb," answered the dealer. "If there is, they buy it. If there isn't, they don't."[65]

During the late 1930s and early 1940s, however, public taste began to shift away from the long, leisurely development of the short story and toward the modern, highly selective, "functional" forms of short fiction. Cobb became aware that his vogue as a fiction writer was waning, and he turned to other kinds of writing, particularly to the job of writing his autobiography. Coming at a time when public acceptance of Cobb's kind of story was still at its height, this transfer of fashion made all of Cobb's fiction appear old-fashioned. It probably accounts for the general lack of interest in Cobb since the 1950s.

Considering the fact that Cobb wrote hundreds of humorous essays, articles, burlesques, and short stories, one cannot hope to deal with all or even most of them in limited space. But the summaries, analyses, and critical commentaries in this chapter are a representative sampling of all the important aspects of Cobb's career as a humorist. If a general assumption can be made about a literary production so large and various, the most enlightening is that it was always a puzzlement to Cobb that his literary reputation appeared to depend not only upon his humorous material but almost exclusively upon the broad and light aspects of that material.

Chapter Five
Old Judge Priest and the Back-Yonder Touch

From the first appearance of Irvin S. Cobb's Old Judge Priest, an "autocratic, bourbon-swilling Kentucky Colonel,"[1] in the *Saturday Evening Post* (11 October 1911), the old judge became the main character in at least forty-two short stories and two short novels.[2] In the first Judge Priest story, Cobb established the main character traits of the old jurist, but story by story the old judge developed unexpected qualities until—despite his simple-seeming exterior—he evolved into the most complex character in Cobb's fiction.

Judge Priest: A Composite from Life

Far from being stultified by the daily stress of newswriting and editing, Cobb was one of the few substantial writers of fiction in America who came to consider their long careers in journalism an asset to their literary careers.[3] In particular, Cobb contended that his most valuable attribute as a fiction writer was the trained reporter's capacity to observe details and to recall them with photographic accuracy and completeness.[4] In his initial concept of old Judge Priest, he used the eye and the ear of the accomplished journalist to create his most memorable character.

According to an eminent Paducah attorney for whose judgment Cobb had considerable respect, the real-life model for old Judge Priest was "a little old county judge who must have been quite a character—or at least he was after Cobb got through writing about him."[5] But in the eyes of the youthful Irvin Cobb, and in the eyes of most residents of Paducah at the turn of the twentieth century, Judge William Sutton Bishop was more than a "character." Known to his familiars as "Billy" Bishop, he was "a tall, portly, slow-moving human being, who always carried a cotton umbrella, wore a well-educated goatee, and white ducks in summer. Bald-headed, florid, poor, with the independence and courage of a lion, he appeared sometimes childish, sometimes masterful, always kind."[6] According to one local historian, Judge Bishop had baby blue eyes and was "without pretense or affectations. He was supposed to be kind, generous to a fault, and completely above pettiness."[7]

Formally, he held the title of "Judge of the First Judicial District of Western Kentucky." Moreover, like many others of his kind who lived in the small southern towns of the era, he was an arbiter of legal entanglements, a confessor to the poor, and in times of trouble, a source of sympathy and homely wisdom. He was also a champion of good liquor, and a genial host who treasured quiet evenings on his front porch, where with his old cronies he swapped stories of bygone days. During Irvin Cobb's boyhood, the lad was unforgettably impressed with the contrasting elements in the character of Judge Bishop. Of these paradoxical elements, none was more intriguing to Cobb's imagination than "the strident, high-pitched voice which, issuing from that globular tenement, made a grotesque contrast, as though a South American tapir had swallowed a tomtit alive and was letting the tomtit do the talking for him" (*EL,* 333). Almost as intriguing, however, was Judge Bishop's double standard of oral expression. He always used a formal vocabulary when he was on the bench, but he lapsed into his native back-yonder dialect as soon as he took off his judicial robes.

Jeff Poindexter: The Ubiquitous Factotum

In the original plan for the tales that have become known as the "Judge Priest" stories, the Protean figure of the old judge was not intended as the central character. At first, Cobb had envisioned as his "hero" the judge's black houseboy and factotum, Jefferson Poindexter. Apparently, Cobb's initial idea was to make of Jeff a clever black retainer in the tradition of the resourceful servant who knows how "to keep his place" while extricating his master from disastrous and seemingly hopeless situations. Under this scheme, Judge Priest and his cronies would have been secondary and tertiary characters who thought of themselves as Jeff's superiors in every way, even if the reader would have recognized them as deluded bumblers whom Jeff repeatedly saved from their bungling.

But as Cobb worked on the earliest of these stories, he found that the judge acquired a life and will of his own. Somehow the ingenious old gentleman thrust himself into the foreground until Cobb let him have his way. Much later, in an access of whimsy, Cobb conjectured that the fault must have been Jeff's. "I just couldn't keep that lazy nigger on the job," he said.[8]

The real-life model for the ubiquitous Jeff Poindexter was one Connie Lee, a black "foot doctor"[9] in Paducah. In 1941, while describing some of the black people who served as models for his characters, Cobb wrote, "Today there is Connie Lee, still the town's leading chiropodist, operating on the old Southern feet of the old Southern families, and the only survivor of all the individuals, white or black, who marched across my manuscripts."[10] Unfortunately, Cobb has never described Connie Lee fully enough to indicate the ways in which Jeff Poindexter resembles his real-life counterpart, nor has any other long-time resident of Paducah done so, though Connie Lee continued to live in Paducah until his death in the spring of 1957.[11]

Fictional Paducahans: Natives and Immigrants

Two of Judge Priest's friends and close companions come often to the judge's home to spend the late afternoons and early evenings in the "porch-yarning" sessions that create a "frame" for many Old Judge Priest stories. The most prominent of these cronies is Dr. Lewis Lake, a gentle, wise, and mellow general practitioner who had served in the Civil War with Judge Priest. The living counterpart of Dr. Lake was Dr. John G. Brooks,[12] who served in the Third Kentucky Regiment under one of Paducah's most famous men, General Lloyd Tilghman. The other member of the storytelling group is a short and portly Civil War veteran called Sergeant Jimmy Bagby, whose characterization is based upon another well-known Kentuckian, William G. Whitefield.

In a number of the Judge Priest stories, Cobb makes use of two German-Jewish immigrants who have established themselves in the community as successful proprietors of a clothing store. Cobb presents them as the Felsburg brothers, Ike and Herman, both of whom came from the "old country." Herman began his career by peddling merchandise from a hand-drawn cart which he had pushed doggedly from house to house on the back roads all over the district.

Altogether unacquainted with the English language, the Felsburg brothers learned their adopted tongue only aurally and experimentally, by picking up a word or a phrase at a time. As a result, they spoke English with thick accents and frequently with only marginal coherence. Coming to America later, after Herman had already established the business, Ike acquired only the most common and necessary English words and phrases. Herman, however, who is more quick-witted and more imaginative than Ike, is capable of creating bizarre malapropisms in his attempts to cope with the vocabulary and syntax of a borrowed language. "The bank was closed tight as a match," he would say, or "Here I am sweating like a tiger," or "A stitch in time is a bird in the hand."[13]

For models of the Felsburg brothers, Cobb used Ullman and Herman Wallerstein, two clothing merchants who were eminent business men in Paducah during Cobb's boyhood. In the early days, most of the financially successful people in Paducah were of Jewish descent,[14] and in creating the Felsburg brothers, Cobb has given his readers an interesting and for the most part a historically reliable picture of the position the Jewish merchant occupied in small Southern towns near the turn of the twentieth century. In doing so, however, Cobb has minimized many of the pejorative ethnic attitudes that prevailed at that time. Instead, he presents the Felsburg brothers sympathetically, though a few of the stories contain fictional townspeople who have a deep-seated hatred of all Jews. Herman Felsburg emerges as a believer in the American democratic philosophy and a devoted supporter of the American system. Cobb usually depicts him not only as an immigrant patriot but also as a unique variety of American hero.[15]

Black Paducahans: Choruses and Bit Players

For minor characters among the black people in the Judge Priest stories, Cobb turned to members of the large Negro community with whom he had become familiar during his childhood. In the opening pages of *Glory, Glory, Hallelujah!*[16] he recalls the "actual personalities" among the black people upon whom he had founded many supporting characters in the Judge Priest stories. Chief among these character types were "'Major Jeems' Williams, as dark-complexioned as Mammoth Cave, and 'Sis' Josephine, his chatty little yellow wife, both of whom advertised themselves as the 'most beatenest team in Dixie at house-cleanin'" (12). Equally important as a model for minor Negro characters was Albert, who in his capacity as head-waiter of the Palmer House in Paducah, "carried, except in the very dead of winter, a palm-leaf fan; carried it even in the hotel dining room, where he used it upon his underlings as a sort of symbolic baton, an evidence of authority"(13–14).

A unique source of information upon members of the black com-

munity in Paducah was the Cobb family's laundress, Aunt Minerva
Victoria Machen. Despite the fact that she was a member of a race who
"can seem to be the most artlessly outspoken and yet, as regards their
own private affairs, remain inwardly the most . . . reticent of all peo-
ples" (15), Aunt Minerva Victoria enjoyed taking Irvin's mother into
intimate confidences concerning the black people of Paducah. Through
his mother, Irvin became vicariously acquainted with several black personages who served as models for Negro characters in his fiction.

Irvin Cobb, Judge Priest, and the "SatEvePost"

The widespread success of the Old Judge Priest stories was in large
measure the outgrowth of Cobb's uncanny ability to find and to be-
friend important publishers like George Horace Lorimer of the *Saturday
Evening Post*. In 1909–10, when Cobb was at the top of his profession
as a newspaper columnist and feature writer, circumstances kept push-
ing him toward a new phase of his career. His daughter "Buff" has
called this shift of direction "the second big break in his career, the
first, of course, being the move from the small town to the big one,
the second, and equally significant one, being his quitting newspaper
work for an attempt to earn his living as a writer of fiction."[17] Torn
between the demon of status quo and the demon of challenge, "he
stewed and he fretted and he worried and longed and hoped and doubt-
ed. . . . When one had to sew and sew and sew again the buttons on
Irvin's vest, and around them appeared a perfectly slick, shiny circle of
cloth worn napless by his unconscious gesture—he was worried."[18]

Samuel "Sam" Blythe was a trusted friend of George Horace Lorimer
and was staff contributor of a widely read political column in the
"SatEvePost." Mrs. Cobb discovered that Sam wanted Irvin to write
fiction, and together they persuaded Cobb to take six weeks' leave from
the *World* in order to give the project his concentrated energies. The
Cobbs took a summer cottage on the shores of Lake Champlain, and to
keep their protégé at work, the Blythes also took a cottage there.
When six weeks had passed, Cobb had written his first piece of fiction,
an eerie short story titled "The Escape of Mr. Trimm."

Cobb marveled at the promptness with which Lorimer bought the
story. He did not know that Blythe had spent considerable time in
convincing Lorimer to take a chance on Cobb, or that Lorimer had
already been favorably impressed by several of Cobb's newspaper features. Neither was Cobb aware that Lorimer had entered upon a cam-

paign to lure promising newspaper writers to the *Post,* as eventually he lured not only Cobb but also such journalistic prodigies as Octavus Roy Cohen, and Ring Lardner.[19] Cobb continued to sell humorous articles to the "SatEvePost," and at last, early in 1911, he gave up his newspaper position to become a staff contributor.

For the next eleven years all the Judge Priest stories appeared in Lorimer's *Post.* During this time Cobb occupied a prominent place in the "Post school of fiction," which included Peter B. Kyne, P. G. Wodehouse, Ring Lardner, Jack London, and most spectacular of all for the devoted readers of the *Post*—Mary Roberts Rinehart, whose friendship with Cobb belied her good-natured war with him in her humorous essay "Isn't That Just Like a Man?" "In Lorimer's inner circle Cobb's wit sparkled as brilliantly as it did in his stories,"[20] says Lorimer's biographer. "Wherever the Lorimer Circle gathered in the old days the globular figure of Cobb could be found, whether at Atlantic City, the [Grand] Canyon, Philadelphia or Palm Springs."[21]

In 1924, however, Ray Long of *Cosmopolitan* conducted a "raid" upon some of the *Post's* most valuable writers. With the financial persuasion of William Randolph Hearst at his disposal, Long offered these writers a three-year contract to write exclusively for *Cosmopolitan,* at salaries exceeding any amounts that Lorimer was willing to meet. So, among others, Peter B. Kyne and Ring Lardner "defected" to *Cosmopolitan,* along with Cobb, who took with him the increasingly popular and lucrative series of tales about Old Judge Priest. Thereafter, most of the Judge Priest stories appeared in *Cosmopolitan,* until Ray Long commissioned the terminal series of tales for *Down Yonder with Judge Priest and Irvin S. Cobb* in 1931–32.

Judge Priest: A Fictional Chronology

Judge William Pitman Priest first appeared in the *Saturday Evening Post* on 28 October 1911. Within a year the same story, "Words and Music," was reprinted as the introductory tale in *Back Home* (1912), which is the first of nine books that are devoted partly or exclusively to stories about old Judge Priest. The series ended with the appearance of *Down Yonder with Judge Priest and Irvin S. Cobb* in 1932.[22]

Because Cobb does not appear to have realized that the Judge Priest stories would grow into so long a series, the early stories became part of the group mostly by mere accumulation. As a result, there is only an incidental chronology among the early stories in *Back Home* and in

Old Judge Priest. Later, in order to account for chronology, Cobb began to weave into some of the stories hints concerning the advancing age of Old Judge Priest. In one or two stories he provided important dates in Judge Priest's fictional life.[23] This kind of internal evidence makes it possible to estimate Judge Priest's age at the time of these events and to determine the intervals between many significant occurrences in the series.

From Cobb's gratuitous hints, one can winnow the information that in 1860, at the age of twenty-one, William Pitman Priest first became a member of the bar; that from 1860 to 1865, when he was between the ages of twenty-one and twenty-six, he served as a Confederate sergeant in the Civil War; and that from 1865 to 1880, when he was between the ages of twenty-six and forty-one, he was in private practice as an attorney-at-law. From 1880 to about 1920—a period of nearly forty years which spanned the ages from forty-one to the late seventies in Judge Priest's life—he served unbroken successive terms as the circuit judge of the First Judicial District of the State of Kentucky. At the time of the last Judge Priest story, he must have been in his mid-eighties, at which time he had retired from law practice altogether.

As far back as the 1890s, a man of forty-seven was hardly beyond the waning years of his prime. Yet, in the first Judge Priest story, Cobb had created a man who appeared to be of advanced age, a man who was remarkable for physical and intellectual energies as well as for enthusiasms that belied his age. This discrepancy is an accident of the evolution of the Judge Priest stories as a series. In fact, the discrepancy suggests that when Cobb wrote his first Judge Priest story he had no idea he was spawning a character that would require continuous development through a long series of interrelated tales.

By 1931–32, while Cobb was writing the stories for the last collection of Judge Priest tales, he managed to contrive for the first time a satisfactory explanation for the discrepancy in the chronology of the series. As the series drew to a close, Cobb apparently realized that the appearance of age in a comparatively young man resides in the universal failure of human beings to perceive age except through a comparison with one's own age. As the narrator of one of the last stories in the series, therefore, he argues the truth of a venerable adage: that an "old" person is and always has been any person who is twenty years older than oneself. "So now, thinking it all over again," says Cobb as his own persona-narrator, "I know how and why it was from the time of my earliest remembrance it always seemed to me that Judge Priest was cushioned with fat and drooped with antiquity. . . . But because I looked upon him with the eyes of childhood he appeared as one already so venerable that soon he must go coasting down hill toward his dotage" (*DY, 27*).

Judge Priest: The Evolution of a Character

During his first few weeks as a staff contributor to the *Saturday Evening Post,* Cobb tested the waters of this new and uncertain phase of his profession by offering his readers a "thriller-chiller"[25] along with some humorous articles and an anonymous series of pieces under the comprehensive title of "On Main Street." He had not offered his editors any of the "back yonder" fiction by which they had expected to create a substantial increase among Southern subscribers. But in the issue of 28 October 1911, the "SatEvePost" published a Cobb story that reeked of "down yonder" southland. It introduced the character of Old Judge Priest, and from that time until the end of the Judge Priest series the curious-minded old judge was Cobb's reliable stock in trade.

Like many of the forty-odd Judge Priest stories that were to follow, "Words and Music" has so simple a plot that it can hardly be considered a story at all save for complications of character development and for conflicts among the characters. Basically the story is a kind of taletelling that was already well known in American fiction—the "courtroom dramas" in which Old Judge Priest is the dominant figure and the prime mover. In the opening pages, Cobb introduces a gallery of "locals" that would appear again and again in the Judge Priest stories: farmers and horse traders, members of the Ladies' Aid Society, an oldtime medical doctor, the town marshall and the county sheriff, the town gallant, the town drunk, and various types of black people who are usually essential to the Judge Priest stories, whether these persons are part of the background or active forces in the tale.

In "Words and Music," a newcomer, Breck Tandy, has killed the most popular man in the county and has hired a Northern lawyer. To the citizens, everything Tandy has done or is supposed to have done seems an unforgiveable affront. Even before the trial begins, the people are convinced that Tandy is guilty. Among the character witnesses for Breck Tandy is one Judge Priest, who once knew Tandy and is convinced that Tandy is being "railroaded." When the old man learns that many of the jurists fought as Confederates in the Civil War, he asks the attorney to put him on the stand as the last witness.

At first, the seemingly senile old man answers questions simply and directly, but at one point he seems to be rambling in his mind as he speaks of the "old days" in 1864, when as a young Confederate soldier he first marched into this town. When the old man mentions almost casually that the father of the accused was marching beside him on that day so long ago, there is an air of palpable sympathy in the courtroom. As the old man says that he had known the prisoner from the boy's babyhood years and that the boy—like his soldier father—has always been manly and honest, through the open windows of the courtroom comes a burst of music from what sounds like a fife and drum. Unknown to the others, Judge Priest has noticed on the streets of the town an old black musician who can imitate the music of any small group, and has hired him to play the marching song of the Confederacy at this strategic moment.

Not surprisingly, the atmosphere in the courtroom changes, especially among the older members of the jury. After only six minutes of deliberation the jury reaches a verdict of innocent, and old Judge Priest leaves the courtroom for the barroom of the Drummer's Home Hotel to partake of something that he calls "nourishment."

The main elements of most Judge Priest stories lie somewhere in "Words and Music." Few of the forty-odd Judge Priest stories introduce new elements altogether. From story to story, however, the judge develops a host of mannerisms that reflect almost infinite variations in his temperament and his state of mind. His plump pinkish face, light blue eyes, and white chin whiskers, for instance, assume every possible change. He uses a variety of little stage properties—his corn cob pipe, steel-rimmed spectacles, false teeth, wrinkled white linen suit, black umbrella, ancient cape overcoat, palm-leaf fan, and hard spectacle case. His short stumpy legs move in every way possible for such legs. Always his high whiny voice proves equal to the occasion, even to sounding clearly above the loudest noises of the largest gatherings of people.

A paradox in the characterization of old Judge Priest is that he is surprisingly agile for a man of his rotundity. When events begin to move toward a climax, the old man may be galvanized into a different being, into a man larger than himself, as he does in one story at the point where he prepares to exhort his old army comrades to act immediately if they are to correct unthinkable wrongs. In this instance, he "reared back, and visibly, before their eyes, his short fat figure lengthened by cubits."[26] As usual in this kind of story, Judge Priest's commanding presence is responsible for the triumph of justice over legal statutes.

One of Judge Priest's most effective devices for influencing other people is his use of deliberate affectation. When he is presiding over the proceedings in his courtroom, or upon any other truly formal occasion, he uses impeccable diction, grammar, and syntax. Upon these occasions he is unmistakably a man of considerable education and good taste. But as soon as he has doffed his judicial robes he consciously becomes a member of the common citizenry, and in this role he uses almost exclusively the diction and the dialect of his native region. As a result, the townspeople consider him and prize him as one of their own.

To Judge Priest, however, this linguistic affectation is not what it may seem. Because he has been a lifelong resident of the town, he has spoken the homely and colloquial dialect of the people from his earliest years. Therefore, the formal and sophisticated language of the courtroom is a mode of communication which he learned much later, when as a young man he underwent the training that is required of successful candidates for jurisprudence degrees. The true affectation in Judge Priest's use of language, then, resides in his adaptation to the formal language of the courtroom, not in his "descending" to the everyday vernacular that he has used from his earliest years among lifelong friends and acquaintances.

In both instances, however, there is something calculated about Judge Priest's alternating two widely disparate levels of communication. He is always careful to select the right shade of speech and dialect for the social occasion that prevails, and, as a result, he has an advantage that gives him singular powers of adaptation. He can function effectively on all levels of society, whether in a small rural town or in the largest of cities. Furthermore, he is perfectly aware of the powers of manipulation and persuasion he has gained thereby, and he is always ready to use these powers when the letter of the law threatens the ascendance of true justice.

A good many of the Judge Priest stories contain episodes in which the old jurist is happily planning or doing one of his two favorite activities, fishing and duck hunting. One of his old friends remarks that the judge will persist in these pursuits as long as he can climb into or out of a boat.[27] In these stories the prediction proves true. With passage of time, though, the judge's mode of transportation undergoes a significant change. During his closing years his reliable white mare, Mittie Mae, dies of old age. Thereafter, instead of traveling to fishing and hunting places in his ancient side-bar buggy, he occupies a seat in Dr. Lake's big touring car.[28]

Judge Priest: The Beneficent Despot

As a politician and a perennial holder of public office, Judge Priest is almost a classic type among rural politicians in the South during the years between the Civil War and the second decade of the twentieth century. Though a man of considerable learning, he understands perfectly the deep distrust of "book learning" that is characteristic of the back-country. While his less perceptive opponents wear themselves out in the "standard" campaign strategies of long speeches to mass assemblies, fierce belaboring of "issues," rhetorical articles in local newspapers, and expensive distribution of leaflets and campaign buttons, Old Judge Priest quietly conducts the seemingly naive "grass-roots" campaigns that have never failed to return him to the bench, term after term.

By the time Judge Priest has been the sole occupant of the circuit judge's chambers through most of his generation and well into the next, he has acquired a widespread reputation as a kind of wizard in legal and political matters. Even the offspring of his generation have heard of his exploits, and when they or their loved ones are in trouble they seek him out, as their parents did before them. In one of the later Judge Priest stories, a troubled young lady reveals to another person the reason why she has turned to Judge Priest for aid in a domestic as well as in a legal and political sense. "Papa always said that when it came to figuring out a political tangle, he was the smartest man he ever saw, nearly. You might not know what he was thinking about but he was thinking hard just the same."[29]

Eventually, Judge Priest becomes a "living legend" in his part of the state. To the general populace of western Kentucky, no less than to his political opponents, he seems possessed of inexplicable powers of perception and of endless ingenuities in the face of adversity. In the political arena, however, except in his own personal campaigns, he always worked behind the scenes, and in a general way he has learned to function so unobtrusively that even his own constituents remain unaware of the scope and power of his influence. Not until he resigns, when he is in his early eighties, do people become aware of his political influence. They realize only in his sudden absence that he has been a kind of "political dictator" all this time. "For upwards of forty years this man had been making slates and running conventions and guiding elections, and . . . his had been almost altogether a one-man machine, a beneficent, single-handed despotism" (*DY*, 246).

To whatever extent Judge Priest may have been a political despot, however, his reasons for being a despot are not those of a tyrant. As both judge and politician he is beyond all else a devoted servant of the public, and he therefore despises no person more wholeheartedly than he despises the flashy, pompous, self-serving public official who uses his office as a patent for his own gain. For such devious, pompous, and self-serving lawyers and politicians as the Honorable Horace Maydew, Judge Priest has only the most profound contempt. Horace Maydew is a classic embodiment of the kind of politician who has dedicated himself to the fabrication of appearances. With the cunning of his kind, he devotes his life to a spurious career of public service. He has created for public view the image of a man whose only care is for the prosperity and the well-being of those who elect him to public office. Somehow he convinces everybody save a perceptive few who—like Judge Priest—know the true character of Horace Maydew. They know him as a morally destitute man of cheap lust and monstrous cupidity who fattens himself upon the public trust.

"His was an uneasy ambition, which ate into him like a canker and gave him no peace," observes an omniscient narrator of one of the Judge Priest stories. "Indeed, peace was not of his craving. He watered his desire with the waters of self-appreciation and mulched it with constant energy, and behold it grew like a gourd."[30] Bloated with his self-importance, Maydew considers himself beyond the common laws of conduct and morality. So he feels not the least twinge of guilt when, with promises of material gain and social standing, he openly steals from honest and self-effacing Lysander Curd the young and nubile wife who has been the joy and the prop of old "Lysandy's" existence.

Though the extraordinary May–December marriage of old Lysander Curd and his girl-wife Luella has seemed to the townfolk a star-crossed yoking from the outset, and though the whole town is aware that Luella Curd and Horace Maydew have been meeting in "secret," Judge Priest is surprised when Lysander confesses that his marriage is to terminate at the earliest date that Judge Priest can arrange by moving the action ahead in the docket. But the Judge's surprise yields to shock when old Lysander makes it clear that in the case of *Curd* v. *Curd* not he the aggrieved husband but Luella the offending wife will be the plaintiff, basing her action on the grounds of drunkenness and nonsupport. Judge Priest is incensed. He knows that Lysander has supported his wife in better circumstances than she has ever known, and above all, that Lysander Curd has never been as much as tipsy in his life. When the Judge levels this accusation at his visitor, old Mr. Curd replies diffidently but firmly, "Well, now . . . you don't know about my private habits, and even if I haven't been drinking in public up to now, that's no sign I'm not fixin' to start in doing so" (*OJ*, 104).

Having made his point, old Lysander Curd leaves Judge Priest snorting indignantly in his chambers. But after a moment of intense reflection, the Judge says aloud to himself, "Under the strict letter of the law I ought to throw this case out of court, I s'pose. But . . . that old man's heart is broke now, and there ain't no earthly reason that I kin think of why that she-devil should be allowed to tromp on the pieces" (*OJ*, 105).

In due time, however, the ties that have bound Mr. and Mrs. Lysander Curd are sundered. Then Mr. Curd retreats to his little farm outside town, and with unseemly haste Mrs. Curd becomes Mrs. State Senator Horace K. Maydew. Meantime, the Senator's greed and ambition have multiplied apace. "If there was a lodge, he joined it . . . if there was an oration to be made he made it. . . . His manner was paternal where it was not fraternal. His eye, though, remained as before—a sharp, greedy, appraising eye" (*OJ*, 112). And so, despite Judge Priest's reputation for redressing wrongs, it appears that he will never be able to put right the grievous injustice of *Curd* v. *Curd*.

But in a seemingly unrelated incident a year or so later, Judge Priest finds a chance to use his best weapons against injustice. Maydew, now a U.S. senatorial candidate, gears up an invincible machine against an aged incumbent. At the convention, Maydew installs his beautiful young wife—the former Mrs. Curd—conspicuously and elegantly in a gilded box above the speaker's platform, like a trophy on display. Judge Priest fights hard against Maydew but seems at last to have given up. Like a beaten man, he leaves the hall.

Outside, he holds secret conferences, and when he returns for the nominations, he humbly withdraws the name of the incumbent. But then he rises unexpectedly to nominate another candidate, whose name he withholds pending a listing of the new candidate's qualifications. In his best back-yonder manner he recommends a man who is humble, honest, and sincere, one who has never hurt another person or destroyed another man's family, one who has never sought or held public office and is therefore uncorrupted by ambition. Thereupon he places in nomination the name of Lysander Curd and demands an alphabetical vote.

All eyes turn at once to the studied opulence of the present Mrs. Maydew in her golden box—and one by one the delegates begin casting their votes for Lysander Curd. Long before the toll is finished, Maydew runs to Judge Priest in humilation, offering to withdraw his name altogether if only the judge will nominate a compromise candidate. So the name of Judge Priest's friend and fellow attorney Dabney Prentiss goes to the convention, and Prentiss delivers the acceptance speech that the judge told him to prepare earlier in the day. Judge Priest knows the weakness of the world's Horace Maydews, and so he wins again.

"Judge Priest Returns" has special interest because it lays the groundwork for two other Judge Priest stories[31] in which the judge defeats Horace and Mrs. Maydew with the same kind of benign manipulation of circumstance. In one story Maydew foments a duel of honor between Judge Priest and a Maydew disciple who is running for office. The judge ignores the challenge for a time, but at the right moment he simply sends his opponent a letter, whereupon the challenger summarily withdraws from both duel and election. The letter contains a portion of the challenger's oath of office, which forbids dueling to any holder of that office.

In the other story, Judge Priest responds to Maydew's demand that Priest withdraw as judge in a certain case, so that Maydew's client cannot suffer from the judge's well-known dislike of Maydew. So Priest obligingly disqualifies himself as judge in this case. But then he becomes the lawyer for Maydew's opponent and soundly defeats Maydew and his obviously guilty client. In a few later stories Maydew rises up to contend against the seemingly dotty old man, but the result is always the same. Of all the lawyers in that judicial district, Maydew is the only one who is not on good terms with old Judge Priest.[32]

At the only point in Judge Priest's long career when he knows he can never in good conscience uphold a newly enacted law, he resigns from the bench. He is nearly eighty when the Volstead Act is passed in "that year of Grace and Drying-up, 1920,"[33] and he finds that, unless he becomes a hypocrite, he cannot enforce the amendment that has inaugurated an era of prohibition against the use of liquor. "Ef I'm not going to abandon my pussonal habits . . . whut am I goin' to do when some poor devil is fetched up before me charged with peddlin' the same stuff that I'm freely imbibin' behind closed doors?" (*DY*, 298).

In the absence of the Volstead Act, however, when any person of legal age could freely patronize saloons, Judge Priest refuses to let his private reverence for good bourbon override his sense of rightness. When six Clay Street ladies come to him for his best advice about keeping a new saloon from encroaching upon their quiet residential neighborhood, he suggests that they can kill the saloon by kindness. They follow his advice that they take turns sitting quietly and pleasantly inside the saloon on the day it opens. They go there, and knitting happily, without complaint or any show of disapproval but only by their staid moral presence, they make customers so self-conscious that one by one they leave and never come back.[34]

In his lifelong crusade to use the law only to achieve true justice, Judge Priest is not beyond applying logical sophistry. In his nearest approach to specious argument, he saves a doomed but morally innocent person by turning legal rhetoric against itself. Since the crime is said to have been committed during a gambling session, everything depends upon specific circumstances of time and place, all of which the testimony has established beyond question. But Priest demonstrates that in the eyes of the law none of the circumstances existed at all. According to a purely technical interpretation of the statutes, he argues, "gamblin' in whatsoever form ain't permitted, recognized, countenanced, nor suffered."[35] Therefore, he concludes, gambling in that state simply does not exist, in which case nobody can have been in that place in order for the crime to be committed; that is, the crime did not occur at all.

But lest Judge Priest be thought a "soft" magistrate who employs his extraordinary talents mostly to exonerate people of crimes, one must not overlook evidence that he works equally hard to bring malefactors to justice. In one story, for example, he makes it clear that he condones and supports capital punishment for those who are guilty of capital crimes, and that he sees no reason to regret those decisions in which he has had to impose that sentence.[36]

In some stories, Judge Priest's mode of thought and behavior is so nearly that of a professional detective that Cobb eventually wrote two short novels which he brings together under the title of *Judge Priest, Detective* (1936–37). Written and published several years after the collection that nominally ended the Judge Priest stories,[37] these two narratives take place shortly after World War I, at the time when "Billy" Priest is in his eighties and retired from the bench.[38]

The focus of the first story is a drowning incident at Reelfoot Lake. Seeing something suspicious during a hearing in which the widow of the drowning victim claims the full estate, Priest fakes a dramatic fainting spell in order to delay proceedings until he can investigate. Thinking of himself as Sherlock Holmes and of his friend Dr. Lake as Dr. Watson, the judge enlists the aid also of his black houseboy, Jeff Poindexter. These three manage to cut through a maze of evidence and to solve a horrifying murder plot in which the "widow" is found to be the supposedly murdered man.

The second of the two stories in *Judge Priest Turns Detective* is not as satisfying. It is, however, a good story in the sentimental vein that Cobb frequently taps and it is a good example of the broad and fervent humanitarianism that informs all Judge Priest stories.

Whatever else he may be, William Pitman Priest is a man whose first and last concern is human values. Through his efforts, a misunderstood and maligned old black woman is taken back into the hearts of those to whom she has devoted her life,[39] some Chicago gangsters are pitted against each other to keep an old fight manager from being cheated,[40] a complete circus parade makes a detour past the house of a little crippled boy,[41] and a deceased white prostitute is given a big funeral in a black church because no white minister will perform the services—and as the procession winds through town, all the derelicts, black and white, join the march to the cemetery.[42]

The Old Soldiers of the Confederacy

In the daily lives of Judge Priest and his people, the memory of the great war between the North and South is a living thing. Judge Priest and his porch-yarning companions were also comrades-in-arms under General Nathan Bedford Forrest in what the judge prefers to call "the army of the Southern Confederacy." To them, Forrest is deified, and the war is a shrine which they must visit and revisit in their memories. There, nothing ever changes. The same stories are told in the same words, the same actions come to life unaltered over the years, and those who tell and hear the old stories take comfort from the repetition. In the first dozen or so retellings, to be sure, the stories had grown by the inevitable embellishments, but after a while they crystallized into ritual, like children's bedtime stories. Sometimes these old soldiers hand a story from one to another, each telling his own segment of the same story.

They had all been young during the war. The man who grew into old Judge Priest had just earned his attorney's license and was known as "Billy" Priest. He had come out of the war with a full head of long, wavy hair, and for his exploits there—never specified but universally acknowledged—he was known as "Fightin' Billy." Then he went into Mexico to fight in the "Maximilian mess."[43] But he got homesick among foreigners and "came tramping up from the Texas border, raggedy as a scarecrow and hungry as a tapeworm" (DY, 32).

By then, Lew Lake had his medical degree and had put up his shingle. So Billy Priest opened his law office on "Legal Row." "Fightin' Billy" Priest eventually became "Old Judge Priest," and Dr. Lewis Lake became "old Doc Lake." They settled down to live their lives and relive the war, along with Sergeant Jimmy Bagby and the others of Gideon K. Irons Camp, U.V.C. (Unreconstructed Veterans of the Confederacy), whose meetings they regularly attended and in which they served long as presiding officers.

These old soldiers figure strongly in many of the Judge Priest tales, especially where matters of honor and responsibility are at stake. A frivolous girl sends thoughtless letters to two brothers who are fighting the war, and their confusion about the intent of the letters creates the town's biggest feud. While the old soldiers are guests of honor on Ladies' Day at the County Fair, one of them prevents a "fixed" trotting race. Well known for his courage and resolve in the war, this man stands by a tree as the racers come around the last bend. In full view of the driver but unseen by the spectators, he aims Jimmy Bagby's rusty and useless old rifle at the culprit, who is a known coward. Instead of winning the race according to the "fix," this faint-hearted bunko artist turns completely off the track and leaves through an open gate in the fence, just as Judge Priest knew he would.[44]

Another old soldier, one of the bravest members of the camp, has not known how to stop the fighting since the war ended. He is found guilty of assault, condemned to two years at hard labor, and finds himself traveling to prison on the same train that is taking members of his camp to a reunion. On the way, he single-handedly subdues two train robbers. As a tribute to the good in him, and purely on his spoken word that he will voluntarily report to prison authorities on the return trip, he is allowed to go on to the reunion with his comrades.[45]

There is also a refreshingly light or at least a whimsical side to many tales in this group of Judge Priest stories. Prizing courage in any man who fought well in the war, these old Confederates are capable of setting aside the otherwise unresolved differences between the Union and the Confederacy. Finding that they have thirteen at table during one of their dinner meetings, for instance, they invite a Union veteran to join them, and their congeniality gains thereby.[46] In all the tales, Old Judge Priest is the moving spirit behind the actions of his comrades. They look to him for leadership, and he never fails them.

J. Poindexter, Col.

However broad of mind and spirit Judge Priest may be, his personal relationship with his black houseboy, Jeff Poindexter, is more antebellum than egalitarian. The attitudes of his creator, Irvin Cobb, however, were tempered by an extraordinary sense of the common lot. Considering the prevailing attitudes of Southern whites toward black people during the first decades of the twentieth century, Cobb's were somewhat more enlightened.

Between Judge Priest and the black folk of the fictional counterpart of Paducah (the contemporary term "black people" would not have been taken kindly then) lay a complex network of social and psychological barriers that could not be entirely breached. The old Judge was fully aware of these barriers and accepted them as regrettable but necessary, even as beneficial, to both races.

But as a thinking man, an extraordinarily sensitive and broad-souled one, he also knew and understood something that too few other white Southerners could accept or wanted to accept. He knew that the highest barriers were not of the white people's making. He understood the reasons why residents of the black community preferred to keep their lives altogether secret from the white community. He knew, too, that this secrecy gave them the advantage of knowing all the closet-skeletons of their white neighbors, while the white folk knew little or nothing about those of the black people.

Reluctance to divulge to Judge Priest the secrets known to his community can amount to downright stubbornness on Jeff Poindexter's part. The idea that any black person could be so foolish as to "inform" upon a white man was enough to terrorize a black Southerner of that time and place. As a last resort, however, a stern man-to-man lecture from the judge usually loosened Jeff's tongue. A typical scolding of this kind occurs when the judge feels it imperative to gain information about a white man whom he suspects of having worse than insincere motives toward a naive young girl of the judge's acquaintance.

"Don't you know more about me than I know about myself?" he asks Jeff with rare directness on this sensitive issue—and it is clearly a rhetorical question. "Don't your people know all the back-alley gossip that's been floatin' 'round durin' the last fifty or seventy-five years in this town? Knowin' it and not furgittin' it, neither."[47] Faced with this outspoken reminder of matters mutually understood but seldom uttered, Jeff confirms the judge's beliefs. As a consequence, the judge is able to blackmail the philanderer into being a good husband to a deserving girl. To any other white man of Jeff's acquaintance, Jeff would not have breathed a syllable of this information. But love, respect, duty, and trust combine to overcome in Jeff his reticence with regard to white folk.

Despite his primary urge to save his own skin at the least hint of any damage to it, Jeff ignores imminent harm and breaks into the judge's bedroom in order to save the old man from the burning house. The timing of this unselfish action, during the evening of a day when Judge Priest has been feeling lonesome for the wife and two daughters long ago lost to a diphtheria epidemic, makes Jeff's devotion all the more precious to an aging man without loved ones.[48]

But for Jeff, physical danger counts for little compared with the supernatural. Anything connected with death or ghosts is enough to make him call upon his feet for purposes of immediate retreat. Even the judge cannot make him stay in the near vicinity of a "haunted" house (JP, 232–41). Yet if he is charged with the errand by his beloved "Jedge," he is capable of climbing a tree that is close enough for him to spy upon a suspected murderer who lives in a sinister old house of most ghastly repute. He forces himself to stay in the tree while he watches the suspect carrying human body-parts into the smokehouse. Contrary to every impulse to flee, and for the sole reason that the judge trusts him to do so, he stays until he sees black smoke coming from the smokehouse chimney (JP, 67–72).

Even on his own, Jeff has remarkable powers to recover from ghost-fright, if he can turn the experience to a personal advantage. Having lost his main lady, Ophelia Stubblefield, to Smooth Crumbaugh, the town bully, a dejected Jeff Poindexter meets face-to-face the "ghost" of Red Hoss Shackleford—and this in a dark street at the moment when funeral ceremonies for this self-same Red Hoss Shackleford are in progress a few blocks away at the Odd Fellows Hall.

Though any sudden confrontation of this kind would normally send Jeff in the opposite direction, he contains himself long enough to learn that Shackleford merely got dead drunk and rolled off a river packet several days' walk from home. With characteristic quickness of wit, Jeff takes him back to the hall and pushes him from the wings onto the platform while the congregation sings the funeral dirge, "Hark! From the Tombs." Upon the appearance of this apparition, Smooth Crumbaugh behaves exactly as Jeff knows he will. Crumbaugh knocks over Ophelia, other people, and benches in a cowardly flight from the hall. Thereupon, Ophelia sees new possibilities in Jeff, who is now the hero of the evening.[49]

Years later, when Judge Priest retires and arranges for Jeff to make his own way in the world, this quick-witted ingenuity accounts for Jeff's rise to eminence above cut-throat competitors in New York City. First, he adopts the ploy of signing himself "J. Poindexter, Col." The abbreviation "Col." is the accepted signature of a Kentucky colonel. To any Northerners who might challenge the designation, Jeff's devious mind has a ready answer. In his case, "Col." means "Colored."

So, as companion to a young white man, Jeff does well for himself in the great metropolis. He guides his young master away from shady oil speculators and scheming women. Then he gets into the booming motion picture industry among the black people of Harlem. When we see him last, he seems to be on his way to the top in a business that should amply reward him for his years of service to the old judge. This part of his life is depicted in Cobb's novel, and to any reader who knows anything of Jeff's previous life, the novel is most entertaining.[50]

The Universal Judge Priest

Even in casual acquaintances among the black people Judge Priest inspires a loyalty beyond anything these folk would think of extending to another white man. On a hunting trip several years after the Civil War, he had occasion to save two of his black acquaintances from mortal harm by the Ku Klux Klan. When a group of Klansmen rode into Judge Priest's camp, he was alone with the two black men whom he had brought along as cook and general man of work. While these two cowered helplessly, the Klan commander avowed his intention to hang them both on the spot. But "Ex-Fightin' Billy" Priest leveled his shotgun at the commander's chest and said, "The fust move you make . . . is goin' to be the signal fur me to blow you ez full of holes ez a flour

sifter. . . . And ef you labor under the fatal delusion that I'm speakin'
idle words, jest lift your little finger—yes, jest stir it enough fur me
to see it stirrin'."[51]

The Klansmen wisely left that corner of the country, and in return
for the favor, "Ex-Fightin' Billy" Priest's two black friends got out a
massive vote of the black folks and elected him to his first political
office as city attorney. Without that last-minute bloc of votes, he could
not have won his first election. This concerted effort on behalf of the
black community appears to indicate something more than gratitude
for Priest's deliverance of two of its members. Their willing espousal
of any white man's political aspirations during their first voting suffer-
ance would seem to bespeak a kind of trust that few if any white men
could garner in the South at that time.

There seems little question that, in creating old Judge Priest, Irvin
Cobb endowed the character with attributes he considered highly admirable. If this assumption be granted, Cobb's nineteenth-century attitudes toward the black people of western Kentucky must have been
liberalized far beyond those of most other white Kentuckians of his
generation. What we know of Cobb's personal relationships with black
acquaintances seems to support this conclusion.

Cobb was always pleased and a little surprised to find that Northern
city dwellers did not tire of the old judge. Having written half-a-dozen
plays, only one of which created any stir,[52] Cobb then worked with
Bayard Veillier to compose a stage adaptation of "Words and Music,"
with other material from *Back Home* and under the title of "Back
Home." It opened at the George M. Cohan Theater in November of
1915, where it met with mixed reviews from critics but was a pleasing
success with patrons.

Nineteen years later the public interest in the old judge remained
high enough that the Twentieth Century-Fox Studios issued a motion
picture version under the title "Judge Priest." Dudley Nicholls and
Lamar Trotti wrote the screenplay, and some of the people in the production could count this effort as a milestone in careers that have become almost legend. The director was John Ford. Will Rogers did the
leading role of Judge Priest, and two of the black character roles were
taken by Stepin Fetchit and Hattie McDaniel, both of whom became
perennials among black actors in Hollywood. A review of the picture
in one of the widely read movie periodicals said that it was not so much
a story as a string of anecdotes "calculated to bring forth laughter and

tears in such rapid succession that you're rather proud of that senti- mental streak in you that you've been hiding so long."[53]

In whatever literary or art form Judge Priest appears, much of his attractiveness as an imaginary character arises from his being a rebel in his calling. His breadth and depth as a human being carry over into his profession and are activated by that profession. He "had no patience with pompous formalities. He never confused law with justice."[54] Moreover, he always defends the under dog: "Even when the under dog is not wholly within the law. . . . [He] respects the law of the land but he recognizes that sometimes technical legalities favor the wrong party. When he is clear about what is right and fair he is willing to give justice a little private guidance in the proper direction."[55] This moral alliance with the Robin Hoods and Zorros of lore and legend gives the character of Old Judge Priest an almost mythic perspective. In America he belongs with all other champions of the common peo- ple, of whatever time or region. In American literature he remains a considerable accomplishment. Though Cobb denied that he wrote for the sake of posterity, Old Judge Priest has lived well beyond his crea- tor's anticipations.

Chapter Six

Tales of the Eerie, the Bizarre, and the Grotesque

In a letter to editor Thomas Costain (12 May 1941), Irvin Cobb suggested that the firm of Doubleday, Doran, consider publishing in one volume "twelve or fifteen of the so-called 'horror yarns' I've done, including such as 'Darkness,' 'The Escape of Mr. Trimm,' 'An Occurrence up a Side Street,' 'The Exit of Anse Dugmore,' 'The Belled Buzzard,' 'One Block from Fifth Avenue,' 'Fishhead,' 'Snake Doctor,' 'The Gallowsmith,' 'Three Wise Men of the East Side,' etc."[1] Later in the same letter, Cobb said of the suggested collection, "Some of these stories had quite a vogue. Some are now forgotten, probably. And some people apparently have forgotten or never knew that I wrote plenty of grim-like blood-and-guts tales in former years."

This collection was never published,[2] but four years later another company published a broader anthology containing eight of these grim stories.[3] The gratuitous interest apparently caused Cobb to reassess his previous assumption, and he expressed pleasure with this evidence that his humorous works had not entirely eclipsed his serious ones.[4]

Cobb felt that he had reason to wonder whether he had been too long pigeonholed as a humorist before he wrote his first piece of outright fiction. That piece was also his first "horror story." That story, "The Escape of Mr. Trimm," appeared in the *Saturday Evening Post* on 27 November 1909 when Cobb was thirty-three and still working on the *Evening World.* By his own admission, this was his favorite among the nearly three hundred short stories he wrote in his lifetime.[5]

Cobb himself has provided the simplest explanation of how and why he began to shift from the comic to the horrifying. In his answer to an epistolary interviewer he once wrote, "I find that when I have written something of a humorous order it gives me an appetite, so to speak, to turn out a nice, gruesome, gory, Edgar-Allan-Poeish kind of tale, and vice-versa."[6] But others have sought more objective reasons for this conjunction of humor and horror. "A strong sense of the grotesque and the whimsical finds material quite as readily in the dark as in the bright sphere of life. It is this feeling of the whimsical that is Irvin Cobb's most precious possession."[7]

The origins of Cobb's penchant for writing "grim-like" tales may have lain farther back in his literary development than he realized at the time when he deliberately set himself the task of writing "The Escape of Mr. Trimm." His most fruitful sources for this kind of story were newspaper accounts and court records, especially when he had some personal involvement with the events. For his first involvement of this kind on a grand scale, one can go all the way back to his "Sourmash" days on the *Louisville Evening Post,* when he had followed the career and eventually the trial of the political demagogue William Goebel and was on the scene of his assassination.

Because Cobb had helped carry the bleeding body from the murder scene, he was able to write his news story as an observer. His closeness to this gory affair made a strong impression upon him, and as one writer observes, "Critics claim the effect of this tragic episode is shown in the occasional stories of horror that Cobb has penned."[8] Though any assumption of this kind must remain speculation, it is difficult to believe that an experience so violent, so bloody, and so early in his career would not have quickened the part of Cobb's creative consciousness that eventually led him to write his "horror" stories.

The speculation gains credibility when it is coupled with the knowledge that Cobb made his first attempt to evoke the grotesque and macabre in a short piece he wrote for the Louisville paper during the time when he also reported the Goebel murder for the same paper. This was a twelve-hundred-word descriptive essay that he later exhumed from a trunk and elaborated into one of his most chilling short stories, "Fishhead."[9]

Cobb's fondness for "The Escape of Mr. Trimm" is understandable. He has explained the origins of this story and the circumstances of its writing more frequently than for any other story he wrote. With passage of time the versions of his account vary in some details, but the main outlines remain constant.[10] The constant factors are these. At some time during 1908–9, while doing one of his regular tasks for the *Evening World,* Cobb found himself among other reporters who were covering the court trial of Charles W. Morse, a flamboyant and high-speculating financier who had run afoul of the law after the "baby panic" of 1907–8. A fearless plunger and superb confidence man, Morse took over his own defense and by endless ploys, ingenious argument, and studied brashness he came near to beating "open-and-shut" charges with which his high-priced lawyers could not seem to cope. He was, however, justifiably sentenced to twelve years in the Atlanta prison. His ability to mold circumstances to his advantage led Cobb to remark to a colleague that such a man could never be kept long in any prison or anywhere under constraint, that nothing would "break him."

With this story in his mind, he one day made a bet with his wife that he could write a piece of fiction without "an intentionally funny line in it," and could sell it to a top fiction market. Though Mrs. Cobb was skeptical, he had great confidence in his idea. He was convinced that the conception of the story was a sure thing even if he proved inadequate in the technical aspects of fiction.

In Cobb's story, the instrument that defeats this clever and powerful man is one of the simplest devices imaginable—a pair of three-dollar disposable handcuffs. Clamped upon his wrists by a slow-witted but practical-minded marshall at the beginning of the train ride to prison, these cheap circlets defy every effort Mr. Trimm makes to foil them. They stay tight through a train wreck from which Mr. Trimm is thrown, otherwise free and entirely unhurt, while the mangled body of another man is identified as his. The cuffs remain through a time of hope when Mr. Trimm speculates that now, in secret, he might be able to get one of his retained lawyers to send him some of his own money for a change of identity and a life of luxury in some foreign country. They stay through the inexorable wearing away of hope as one by one each more desperate effort fails. They stay and even tighten on his bloody, mangled wrists through a slow but steady moral and physical disintegration. They are there when, disheveled and starved and sick and utterly abject, he almost eagerly gives himself up to a country constable.

Cobb was right. The elements of the story are those of one of the most reliable of all short story lines. Moreover, Cobb's painstaking development of concrete details and his careful management of the mounting action gave every evidence that he had a high aptitude for fiction writing. There is an account to the effect that, under the title "The Grip of the Law," he first offered the story to *Everybody's Magazine*. There, editor Theodore Dreiser rejected it, not because he did not like it, but because he did not want to offend his publisher, who had once been a business partner with Morse.[11] At any rate, the *Saturday Evening Post* took it immediately, and as Cobb remarks, "I won my bet, and gave up earning an honest living as a newspaper reporter and turned fiction writer."[12]

Tales of Terror and Pathos

When Cobb turned the true story of Charles W. Morse into fiction, the most unsavory aspects of Morse became submerged in the character of the wealthy Mr. Trimm, in whom prevailed the traits of monumental cleverness and supreme self-confidence. As a result of the transfiguration, Mr. Trimm becomes a person who is capable of evoking a degree of sympathy that his real-life model could not. As terror mounts in him, and after almost superhuman endurance he gives way to despair, he becomes increasingly pathetic. In varying combinations and degrees, Cobb uses these elements in half a dozen other stories, some of which, like "The Escape of Mr. Trimm," are among his best.

Cobb had an extraordinary talent for creating fictional settings that are so eerie and bizarre as to cause pathos to arise from something that borders upon or becomes part of terror itself. None of his stories accomplishes this ascendance more effectively than does "The Great Auk."[13] Cobb got the idea for the story from sportswriter Bozeman Bulger, who told him about an old actor who went around declaring that he had spent the day at the seashore. The truth was that this old trouper lived in a deserted theater and had begun to live according to illusions that were impressed upon his mind by exotic scenes painted on the old backdrops.[14]

Bulger thought the idea comic, but to Cobb, with his abiding interest in the theater, the plight of the old actor seemed most sorrowful. Having worked with theater people, Cobb knew that the golden age of versatile repertory acting had yielded to the specialists, to actors who were trained for only one kind of part. This "cracked" anachronism of a bygone time suggested to Cobb's imagination a great repertory actor who had become in his own sphere of life an extinct species like the Great Auk.

For the sake of his story, Cobb conceives the characters of a young playwright and a somewhat older director who have been looking vainly for an actor to play a grandfather role. Remembering one of the best of the actors who a quarter-century ago had been able to perform all kinds of parts, the director takes the playwright to an abandoned, forgotten theater far downtown. Inside, they find themselves among eerie and unwholesome surroundings. "The place looked dead and smelled dead and was dead. . . . heavy-laden with boneyard scents—rot and corrosion and rust and dust . . . taints of moulded leather and gangrened metal, of wormgnawed woodwork and moth-eaten fabrics" (227).

In this mausoleum of the dramatic art the old actor appears on a derelict stage where, with consummate brilliance, he performs one classic scene after another, taking all parts. Though he plays as if to a full house, the only visible spectator is a little gutter-gamin who claps and whistles wildly at the performance. For so doing, he has the privilege of sleeping in the theater on cold nights. The two hidden spectators agree that no other actor could do their grandfather part remotely as well as this "Great Auk" of the stage world. But they understand also that the old actor is hopelessly insane. "Every haunted house is entitled to its ghost," says the director (243). So they leave an old actor to his haunts.

In "Darkness,"[15] also, pathos is the outgrowth of an interaction between a sympathetic character, Dudley Stackpole, and surroundings that are so eerie and bizarre as to inspire horror. At the Stackpole mill, Dudley had once been forced into an unequal and unsought gunfight. In the confrontation, one of the Tatum brothers had been shot and killed, and Dudley had been acquitted as having acted in unavoidable self-defense. Thereafter, Stackpole has lived in obsessive fear of darkness, convinced that in the dark his imagination will conjure up Tatum's agonized face. In his house, the lights always burn in all the rooms. He sleeps fitfully and only in the brightest possible light. He leaves the house only in broad daylight. He wears only sad-toned clothing. The skin of his face has become the color and texture of an abandoned hornet's nest. He rarely speaks to anybody: "He would make you think of a man molded out of a fog; almost he was a man made of smoke" (15).

One day a dying man in a faraway town confesses that he, not Stackpole, had killed Tatum. An old enemy of the Tatums, this man took advantage of the confusion at the mill to hide and kill Tatum. Now Stackpole can sleep again in comforting darkness. He can become the normal, happy, social being he once was. But the people of the town do not react accordingly.

They have become accustomed to Stackpole as he has been all these years. They resent what seems to them unwarranted familiarity when he speaks to them. They behave as though he is depriving them of something when he is no longer the Dudley Stackpole who has become the town character. Worst of all, the safe, comforting, concealing darkness he has yearned for is now an enemy in itself. As soon as he turns out the lights at night, he is stricken with a nameless horror of the darkness merely as darkness. It smothers. Unable to bear the darkness or to live longer in ceaseless bright light, he turns on the gas to find peace only in death.

Cobb's awareness of the dark as a common property of terror is borne out by another story, "Blacker Than Sin,"[16] in which he uses blackness to instill in his readers an almost overweening sense of horror. In this story, however, the setting is not the source of the horror, as in "The Great Auk." It arises here from the contrast between the normalcy of everyday life in a small Southern town and the sinister blackness of a woman's daily costume.

The main line of the story is this. One Major Foxmaster has appeared in a rather sleepy little town, and after a considerable time he has succeeded in becoming accepted by the residents. But one day a small, erect, slender woman appears there also. Dressed from top of head to the ground in a black dress and veil, she begins to follow the major everywhere he goes. She moves soundlessly and seemingly without movement, as though she floats rather than walks. She never speaks to the major or to anyone. She never interferes with him in any way. But she is always there. Though her identity is a mystery in the town, rumor says that the major had wronged her and abandoned her as a young girl, that everywhere he has fled she finds him, to get her vengeance in this way.

The imagination of the town is fired by her presence, and the people speculate endlessly about her. But the major never acknowledges her presence. He goes his way as if she does not exist. He does so, that is, until he has grown old and stooped and his step has become an old man's step. Then he realizes that the woman in black seems unchanged by the years. Still she floats behind him, straight and strong as on the day he wronged her. Now he begins thinking her a supernatural avenger. At length he loses his composure. He whirls upon her in the public street. He tears away her veil, staggers backward, clutches at his chest. Behind the veil he has seen a face as black as the Pit—"Blacker Than Sin." And he has fallen dead of sudden heart stoppage.

Only then does the town have its answer. The real avenger had come there, but she had died some time ago. Upon her death she had altered her will to the effect that her young black housemaid would perpetuate the major's torment until he expired, whereupon the maid would legally inherit her mistress' considerable estate.

This story is better crafted than are the previous ones. In it there is less padding, less authorial philosophizing, and the climactic disclosure is managed cleanly and convincingly. It is an austere story, for which it is the more effective.

"The Exit of Anse Dugmore" is essentially a revenge story in which the act of revenge takes a strange, unexpected, and sentimental turn. When Anse Dugmore, the central character, shoots and kills one of the Tranthams in a feud, he is sentenced to life at hard labor. Within four years, he is so far gone with consumption that the governor sets him free to die at home. There he finds that his wife has taken his two little boys and has "gone over" to Wyatt Trantham, who is now head of the enemy clan.

To most of the other people in the story it seems that Anse Dugmore "never had any more feelings than a moccasin snake" (191), but the truth is that his "dumb, unuttered love" (195) for his two boys is the only thing that has kept him alive at all. Slowly coughing up his life's blood, he drags himself to a hillside above the main trail and lies in ambush for Wyatt Trantham to ride his mule home from Christmas shopping in the town. When the time comes, knowing that he has only life enough to pull the trigger, Anse brings his rifle sight to rest on his enemy's chest and begins to squeeze the trigger. At the same instant, Wyatt takes a toy drum from his saddle bags, and Anse can also see sacks of Christmas candy and other gifts of the kind loved by little boys. As Trantham looks at the Christmas presents, he hears a long, gurgling sigh from the hillside, and then goes on his way. When searchers find the body of Anse Dugmore, his finger is still tight against the trigger.

Though Cobb's sentimentality is as obvious as his fondness for contrivances, he does succeed in making Anse Dugmore believable, pathetic, and even admirable—evidence of considerable competence in the storytelling craft.

In "The Gallowsmith," however, Cobb manages a transformation as unlikely as that of Anse Dugmore, and he does it more convincingly. It is a story based upon the potentially devastating effects of a suddenly awakened imagination in a man who never knew he had one, and in whose profession no man can allow himself to have one. His calling is that of public hangman.

At sixty-five or so, Jacob Dramm appears to have all the best qualities for a man in so melancholy a profession. His only physical restriction is a long-standing heart condition, but in compensation he is by nature unexcitable, methodical, meticulous with detail, and beyond everything else literal and practical of mind. He averages twelve executions a year and is well satisfied that he has accomplished each with maximum efficiency and minimum discomfort to the condemned. When one execution is over, it is a job well done and entirely out of mind. He considers himself a respectable officer of the state.

But the time comes when a hard and arrogant desperado refuses to accept his doom as others have done. While the gallowsmith makes his routine preparations, the condemned man lays a curse upon him. He, the criminal, will come back to haunt his hangman, and he will take his soul to hell along with his own. For Jacob Dramm, this is a new and disturbing experience. He is unaware that he is hurrying his procedure. As a consequence, the man does not die instantly with a broken neck. He dangles at the end of the rope, slowly strangling. The whole body writhes and jerks in what seems demonic gyrations. The crimson glow of the just-risen sun projects this Devil's dance upon the prison wall, and the image burns itself into the mind of the hangman.

The event has awakened in Jacob Dramm an unknown faculty—that of the imagination. Never having had one, he finds it uncontrollable. All day he wanders the streets in torment. Back home, late at night, he steps on and only half kills a deformed mouse that has crawled in from outside. Still disturbed, he partially raises the blind and absentmindedly tosses the mouse through the open window. Then, lying alone in the sinister darkness, his imagination playing and replaying the awful scene of the morning, he is transfixed by something he sees through the window. The frame is filled with a brilliant, flickering crimson light. In that square is a dangling figure, kicking and writhing in eternal torment.

Next morning the sheriff finds Dramm's corpse lying in the bed. The hangman's heart has stopped and there is terror on his face. Outside the window, in a neighbor's yard, a pile of autumn leaves is still smoldering. In the window frame dangles the body of a deformed mouse, its tail tangled in the sashcord.

Aside from its almost too-heavy reliance upon coincidence at the conclusion, this tale is a startling excursion into the fictional use of the psychology of terror. From the opening paragraph it builds upon the sinister occupation of the hero and upon his believable if almost subhuman detachment from its implications. As a result, the unexpected and rampant emergence of an uncontrollable imagination is a fearful thing. This story is probably the best in a group of Cobb's tales that have in common some degree of horror, and with whose central characters one is likely to be sympathetic.

Tales of Terror and the Grotesque

In another group of Cobb's "horror" tales, the central characters tend to be malefactors or utter grotesques. Some are a bit of both. By and large, they are not persons for whom most people are likely to feel sympathy.

Among these stories "The Belled Buzzard" (*E,* 54–76) is the least satisfactory from a technical point of view. But it is also the most widely celebrated. In this story Squire Gathers, an old man with a young wife, has shot and killed a young itinerant whom the squire suspects of philandering with his wife. Leaving the murder gun and the body where they may not be found for years, the old man is satisfied with his work and goes his way ostensibly without fear or qualm of conscience. However, as in Poe's "Telltale Heart," the murderer's conscience will not be still. The deus ex machina is a buzzard, supposedly carrying a never silent cowbell. It circles incessantly over the squire's house, sounding the bell and driving the murderer almost insane. At the end of the story, someone stumbles upon the body of the murdered man and the authorities arrange a coroner's inquest. As a justice of the peace, the squire is called upon to conduct the proceedings. There, with the body of his victim upon display, he manages to keep a cool demeanor. But now he hears again the sound of the bell. It comes closer and closer, until it seems to be outside the door of the inquest room. At this point the squire breaks. In an instant he is utterly insane. He throws himself upon the floor, confessing his guilt over and over. The door opens, and into the room walks a little boy. He is ringing a cowbell he has found somewhere and has appropriated as a toy.

A far better use of the psychological power of local superstition appears in "Snake Doctor."[17] In this story, the superstition holds that the dragonfly—known in the North as the devil's darning needle—is a malign insect that ministers to ailing moccasin snakes. It is known therefore as the snake doctor. By a similar association, the titular character in the story is known in his locality as Snake Doctor. Rives by name, this man is a grotesque whose appearance and movements are peculiarly snakelike. Moreover, he lives alone in the middle of a dense and tangled area where snakes abound. He makes his living by catching them in order to sell their skins and the oils he renders from them. He is regarded as a friend and even kin to the snakes. In return, they protect him from harm. He is thought, also, to have a fortune hidden in his cabin, with a pet snake to guard it.

The action of the story is rapid and complicated, but the basic sequence of events is this. An avaricious neighbor erroneously suspects his wife of cohabiting with Snake Doctor, though she is really a kindhearted soul who goes to Snake Doctor's cabin once a day to tend him in a sickness. So the husband contrives an intricate and seemingly foolproof plan to kill Snake Doctor and steal his money without implicating himself. But he shoots his wife by mistake and finds himself in the dark cabin, searching for the cache of money.

He thrusts his hand into a hole in the cabin wall. At the same instant he dimly sees there the head of a snake. In horror he withdraws his hand but feels a stab of pain on a fingertip. Fang marks! Blindly he runs from the cabin. But in the tangled weeds outside the cabin he dies slowly and in great pain, feeling every symptom of snake bite. An attending physician, however, says that he has never known a human being to actually die from the bite of a moccasin snake. In the cabin, Snake Doctor's "fortune" of ninety-seven dollars remains untouched inside a hole in the wall, a hole that is lined with coils of barbed wire and guarded by a stuffed snake, posed as if to strike. The story won the O. Henry Memorial Award as the best short story published in 1922.[18]

"January Thaw"[19] is basically a simpler story. But the tissue of the scheme contrived by the murderer is extraordinarily fragile, and the horror that arises from the failure of his plan creates in him a much slower and more tortuous form of disintegration. Before murdering his partner in crime, a man named Champney works out a "foolproof" plan for disposing of the corpse. The two men have hidden out during the winter in one of the northeastern villages where people come to ski. According to local custom, most visitors have built across an open slope all kinds of grotesque sculptures made of snow. Feeling clever and superior, Champney has propped up his partner's corpse and built a snow sculpture around it. Now it appears to be merely another of the countless snow statues that decorate the slope.

Returning to his rooming house at the edge of the slope after he has concealed the corpse, the murderer breaks his leg on some ice and must stay in the house until it mends. He is in no hurry, since old-timers have said that the snow stays late into the spring. But Champney has not been told of a very short interval called the "January thaw." This quick thawing frequently melts all the snow before the regular winter season resumes. So Champney sits looking helplessly through his window for a whole day while the snow turns to slush. In mounting terror he stares while the snow covering drips from the body of his victim. By nightfall he knows what every person in the village will see the next morning. In the dark, he drags his broken leg across the slope. But his solicitous landlord finds him gone, follows his trail onto the slope, and finds him crouched at the base of a melting statue. Possessed by an insane compulsion, Champney is scooping up armfuls of slush and trying to plaster it back upon the stark white legs of a propped-up corpse.

The "purest" of all Cobb's horror stories, however, is "An Occurrence up a Side Street" (E, 79–95). Though Cobb has spoken of his penchant for turning from humor to a "Poe-ish" kind of tale, and though many critics and reviewers have compared his "horror" stories to those of Poe, this is Cobb's only story to have something of the structure as well as the flavor of Poe. The main reason the story justifies this comparison is that when Cobb selected the essential ingredients for the story he pared away everything else in order to focus upon the moment of horror. This moment is the brief span of time that begins after the sense of horror has become intolerable to the characters. It ends only with the catastrophe to which the horror has been building.

"An Occurrence up a Side Street" is one of Cobb's earliest attempts to write fiction. He found inspiration for the story in newspaper accounts of a bizarre contemporary murder case. According to these accounts, the two culprits, a man and a woman, committed murder—a most gory and messy one—in the bathroom of a downtown flat. Then they find that there is no safe hiding place except the last place anybody might think to look, in the apartment itself. The police have completed their investigation and have removed the body. But they have sealed the door and placed a guard in the street outside, so that none of the evidence can be disturbed. The murderers have gained entry through a rear cellar window that is known only to them. Here they are, then, prisoners at the scene of their own worst nightmare, with the corpse gone but all the gore remaining.

To Cobb's credit, he appears to have realized—better than with any other story he wrote—that the tale he wanted to tell was confined entirely within the walls of that apartment. Accordingly, "An Occurrence up a Side Street" begins and ends there, with only a "flashback" or two for explanation of necessary background.

The city is in the grip of a heat wave. Because the prisoners cannot open windows without disclosing their presence to the guard on the street below, the apartment is stifling. The man sits at a table peeling an overripe peach. The woman moves constantly back and forth to the window to see whether the policeman is still on guard. In the heat of the night, the odor of the peach seems heavy and oversweet and sticky. Upon the closed white bathroom door are thousands of fat, buzzing, green-bodied flies. In a heavy clump they have clustered upon the white porcelain door-knob and around the keyhole, where they are "forever cleaning their shiny wings and rubbing the ends of their fore-legs together with the loathsome suggestion of little gravediggers anointing their palms" (*E,* 88).

Having conspired to commit an unspeakable crime so that they can be together, the two lovers are now "stuck" with each other. They are alone against the world, with nothing in common save the thing they most loath. Now they loath each other and want nothing more than to be rid of each other. So the man has a motive in peeling an overripe peach, just as the woman has one in her prowling across the room behind his chair. She wants to keep him in front of her, and in view at all times. But in a rare moment when she is watching something out-side, he pours two glasses of cheap, warm champagne. Into her glass, he drops a liquid that has a strong peach odor. At the same time, he breaks open the pit of the peach. Unaware of what he has done, but seeing her chance, the woman steps behind him and plunges into his eye a ten-inch hatpin. He dies instantly, and with hardly any blood. She notices a glass of champagne on the table, and in a surge of relief she tosses it down, sensing the strong smell of peach but thinking it the broken peach pit. She falls dead beside him.

Despite the wrenching contrivance, "An Occurrence up a Side Street" is Cobb's best story. His focus upon the crucial situation elim-inates his usual philosophical excursions and his tendency to over-elaborate contributing circumstances. Since the horror has been building for a considerable time before the opening paragraphs, Cobb is able to plunge directly into the stream and to develop the sense of horror with a fullness and impact that his other stories do not achieve. All in all, Cobb has brought to this story a discipline and a focus unusual in his fiction.

One other tale belongs in this group, though it is unlike the rest of Cobb's "horror" stories. The story is "Fishhead" (*E,* 242–57). Its substance is not folklore in the ordinary sense, though some form of folklore is an important element in the story. The world of "Fishhead" lies in some borderland where folklore and natural history meet the supernatural. There is something in it, too, of the kind of mythology that builds tales around creatures that are part man and part animal, but belonging to neither species.

The freak of nature known as "Fishhead" seems more fish than man. Though his natural element is air, though he walks erect, though he lives as a man lives—in a shack at the edge of a stagnant bayou of Reelfoot Lake—he seems otherwise a nearer kin to the monstrous and obscene catfish indigenous to those waters: "His skull sloped backward so abruptly that he could hardly be said to have a forehead at all; his chin slanted off right into nothing. His eyes were small and round with shallow, glazed, pale-yellow pupils, and they were set wide apart in his head and they were unwinking and staring, like a fish's eyes. His nose was no more than a pair of tiny slits in the middle of the yellow mask. His mouth was the worst of all. It was the awful mouth of a catfish, lipless and almost inconceivably wide, stretching from side to side" (*E,* 247). According to the lore of the lake, his mother had been frightened by one of the big fish before he was born.

It is said that these big fish are Fishhead's only friends, for people fear him, especially at night, when he swims and cavorts with the fish and even feeds with them, eating whatever they eat. At sunset he always walks barefoot to the end of a huge fallen tree that extends far out into the deep water, and there he squats in the dark. According to local superstition, a strange booming sound that carries across the lake is the cry that Fishhead makes to call the big fish to his log at sundown.

The two Baxter boys have pledged themselves to murder Fishhead in revenge for a beating that Fishhead had once given them. One day at sundown they come secretly, paddling a pirogue, to shoot him when he comes to the end of his log. They stand in their boat and fire from behind another fallen tree. But the recoil of the gun knocks them into the water. Mortally hit by a load of heavy buckshot, Fishhead is able to make his great, booming cry before he slips quietly into the water.

Neither of the Baxter boys is ever seen again. The big fish have come to Fishhead's call, and they have pulled the murderers to the bottom of the lake.

"Fishhead" is more an expanded incident than a short story. Yet it has the fullness of substance and characterization that are necessary to a short story, and it has all the impact of a short story. Its hybrid form is probably the result of its being expanded from a short descriptive essay for a newspaper column. At any rate, it is in a unique fashion the eeriest, the most grotesque, and the most horrifying of all Cobb's fictional narratives.

Stories of Complication and Suspense

Among the "horror" stories that Cobb mentions in his letter to Costain is "Three Wise Men of the East Side."[20] In several important ways, however, it does not appear to belong with the genuine horror tales. Like some other stories by Cobb, the main element in them is not so much horror as complication of plot and the building of suspense.

A category of marginal "horror" tales might include such stories as "The Luck Piece"[21] and "Faith, Hope and Charity"[22] along with "Three Wise Men of the East Side." All of them are eerie. Each contains a moment of real terror, but the moment is for the most part unsustained, so that the terror develops mostly as a by-product of involved action. In some instances, terror is at best incidental to most other elements of the story.

"The Luck Piece," for instance, opens with fast action that leads to an eerie struggle during which the hero-figure accidentally shoots and kills a man who wants to kill him. This action occurs in a dark alley, late at night, just before the crowds begin to leave the theaters a block or so away on Broadway. Beyond this episode, the protagonist's urgent flight from the police could become terrifying. But terror is dissipated in a contest of wits between the murderer and a wily old detective who knows the culprit's mind and habits, and whom the culprit fears therefore above all.

"Three Wise Men of the East Side" is a complicated death-row story of mutual double- and triple-cross. There is always horror in a man's waiting for his own execution, but in this story, the horror has been resolved almost before the story opens. It has been preempted by the one-upmanship of the condemned man's plot to choose his own time

and method of death. Further, even the horror of suicide is mitigated
by the sense of victory that comes with his foiling the authorities.

He bribes his lawyer to smuggle in a cyanide pill that he can swallow
just before he goes to the death chamber. He also bribes a guard to
slip it to him at the chosen moment. But the guard gives him a fake
pill, a harmless one. The condemned man has a few moments of intense
horror as he realizes that the pill has not worked and that he must die
in the electric chair. But afterward the lawyer finds that the "reward"
in the bank vault is only burglar tools, and the guard finds that his
$1,000 bribe is counterfeit.

Similarly, in "Faith, Hope and Charity" each of three prisoners has
a morbid fear of dying in the way his country has condemned him to
die. A Frenchman has a horror of dying by the guillotine; a Spaniard
by the garotte; an Italian by live burial. Together they escape from a
train in the Sonoran Desert of Mexico, and each goes his own way. But
in their flight, the Frenchman is accidentally beheaded by a malfunc-
tioning elevator, the Spaniard is accidentally garotted by the shrinking
of rawhide around his neck, and the Italian is accidentally buried alive
in a box canyon.

The three stories are grounded in horror, and horror remains in them
as a kind of threat. But the horror is metamorphic. Instead of mater-
ializing in its own form, it becomes urgency of survival, complicated
scheming, hurried action. Horror ceases to be the main ingredient and
becomes the means by which emerges one of Cobb's favorite effects—
a combination of irony and grim humor.

A Peculiar Horror

Cobb had good reason to suggest that his "so-called" horror stories
be collected and published together. They constitute an extraordinary
anthology of a kind that seems always to have found readers. It would
be unfortunate, however, if these stories were to be advanced as Irvin
Cobb's answer to Edgar Allan Poe. There is little in them of "the misty
mid region of Weir," of the broody supernatural madness that pervades
"The Fall of the House of Usher," or of the glooming cavern-world of
"The Cask of Amontillado." Save for the grotesque biologic mutation
called "Fishhead," Cobb's people are caught up in the affairs of everyday living. They are in this world and of this world, and their horrors
are recognizable as the depths into which worldly affairs can plunge

those who are susceptible to bizarre and outré circumstance. The result is a peculiar horror that belongs only to Cobb.

The typical summary of Cobb's horror tales is that "Nothing better can be found in Poe's collected works. One is impressed not only with the beauty and simplicity of his prose, but with the tremendous power of his tragic conceptions and his art in dealing with terror."[23] Such generalized references as this have diverted later commentators from searching out the real qualities of his horror tales and from attempts to discover more defensible reasons for their effectiveness.

For reasons yet more obscure and disturbing, the impact of Cobb's "horror" stories upon readers of his day has come from the tales that are least good from a technical standpoint. It is difficult to understand why "The Belled Buzzard" was an overwhelming success with the general reading public during the decades when the other "horror" tales were appearing in the magazines. But this story appears to have been a favorite, and this kind of critical thinking has hindered development of more defensible attitudes toward all of Cobb's fiction.

A few cooler heads have appeared, but they have not prevailed. Sloane Gordon, for instance, perceived the dichotomies of public taste in this regard, and he wrote, "The critical public has voted his 'The Belled Buzzard' as Cobb's best effort. There are lots of people who don't think so. But Cobb himself likes it immensely. It has been compared to some of Poe's most shuddery productions. It doesn't compare with them. But it's a corking story."[24] In this kind of assessment lies something nearer the truth about the remarkable "horror" stories of Irvin Cobb. They are probably better stories than most students of the genre have realized.

Chapter Seven
What Is the End of Anything?

For Irvin Cobb, the "big" years extended roughly from the end of World War I to the financial "crash" of 1929. During this period he felt comfortable in the name he had made for himself as a newspaperman and after-dinner speaker. The Judge Priest tales were sweeping the country, and Cobb's reputation as humorist was high and increasing. As a writer of general fiction he was going almost indiscriminately from tales of horror to realistic ones about city life—lost souls, con men, gangsters, egomaniacs—to sentimental ones, and on through harsh or romantic ones about the American West. He sold everything he wrote. The family was on "easy street."

With *J. Poindexter, Colored* (1922), *Alias Ben Alibi* (1925), *Chivalry Peak* (1927), and *Red Likker* (1929) he tried his hand at novel writing, but in this he met with lukewarm success. Later, in the 1930s, he tried again with *Murder Day By Day* (1933), which found a strongly mixed reaction, and with *Judge Priest Turns Detective* (1936–37), which was accepted as the last link in a saga that was ready to end, and did.

Red Likker, however, gave Cobb the lasting distinction of having written the only novel about the long rise of the "Bourbon Aristocracy" in Kentucky and of its decline into genteel respectability after Prohibition. With this distinction, Cobb earned the particular affection of all Southerners to whom the "Bourbon Aristocracy" has remained a cherished institution.[1] Elsewhere, however, it is little remembered.

Alias Ben Alibi is also a book that deserves better than the almost total obscurity into which it has fallen. It is a series of interconnected characters and episodes that become one of the sharpest and most nearly authentic fictional studies of American newspapermen working under an editor whose discipline and dedication are the outgrowth of a personality far more subtle and complex than that of the stereotyped "hard-nosed" editor.

For the Cobbs, a downhill slide began with the "dark" times just before and after 1929. By the late 1920s Cobb's brand of storytelling had begun to go out of fashion. The leisurely, rambling, anecdotal style of which he had become an acknowledged master was yielding to that of young writers like Ernest Hemingway, whose graphic economy of word and phrase in *The Sun Also Rises* (1926) eventually became the "style-making mastery of the art of modern narration"[2] that was more to the taste of American readers into the middle of the twentieth century and beyond. Cobb had to face the changing times, and his reluctant acceptance of the change was devastating to everything he had made his own.

For over twenty years, comparatively late in life, he had been writing "a new story, out of his head, month after month, year after year, that kept the whole glittering, swirling accumulation together,"[3] says Elisabeth Cobb of the incredible literary output that had kept the family in property, automobiles, and all the comfortable things of their estate. So he became restless, and because he did not know what to do with himself, he floundered. When the banks failed in the fall of 1929, much of the family reserves were lost, and "suddenly he could not write any more short stories. That was all there was to it. He did not have any more short stories left in his system."[4]

At about this time, however, the Judge Priest movie was nearing production in California, and Hal Roach invited Cobb to Hollywood to work with him on some short pictures. After considerable fretting, Cobb decided that any future he had left seemed brighter in California than it did anywhere else. Many of his old friends were there, especially Will Rogers, for whom Cobb had an abiding affection. Once more, he picked up his family and moved, this time to Los Angeles, where he installed them in a spacious and comfortable house at 1717 San Vicente Boulevard.

Here he stayed for the fifteen years or so that were left to him. He came a famous man, almost a living legend, like many other living legends who were in the glamour capital searching for brilliant endings to illustrious but fading careers. He enjoyed being on the production set as advisor for the Judge Priest movie. He worked on a good many other pictures, a little writing here, some acting there. But to his keen disappointment he never had the success he had envisioned for himself in the motion picture business. He found the process of movie-making fascinating, however, and directors liked to work with him because he always supplied some of the funniest lines—usually impromptu or ad lib.

He derived particular pleasure from working with Will Rogers, and his most notable success as an actor was in the role of a steamboat captain in *Steamboat 'Round the Bend* (1935). Rogers had suggested that he and Cobb should team up as rival riverboat captains conducting a grudge-race down the Mississippi to New Orleans. Cobb liked the idea and had great fun playing the corpulent captain of *The Pride of Paducah*. This is the only movie of Cobb's that has been brought back for television reruns in the past few decades.

Within his first few years in Hollywood, he had established much the same reputation in the community that he had enjoyed in New York. Though unable to write with his former energy, he did not allow his writing to languish. Besides a good many movie scripts he managed to produce two full-size novels, two short novels, a great many articles, and a regular syndicated newspaper column. But he was feeling the first symptoms of chronic illness, and depressing events kept piling up. He lost Will Hogg, whose friendship had always been to him a rocklike refuge. Then it was Will Rogers, who died in an airplane crash with Wiley Post and left in Cobb the sense of aloneness that Hollywood has always intensified beyond hope and reason. The most stunning blow came from the newspaper syndicate, which canceled his column in a most summary and impersonal way, without courtesy of explanation.

Exit Laughing

When one considers Cobb's circumstances at this juncture, it seems that the writing of his memoirs was the most obvious course for him to take. He was sixty-four years old and could no longer deny himself the admission that he was in ill health. Publishers appeared ready for the enterprise. Besides, everybody else of any consequence seemed to be writing memoirs, and despite his innate modesty about his accomplishments, he knew that his life had given him things worth writing about.

Further, he justified his autobiography, *Exit Laughing,* by means of some practical and convincing arguments. For more than forty years, he reminded his readers, he had traveled the world to write about people, things, and events, including cataclysmic ones like the two world wars. Writing had been his lifelong business and was now an ingrained habit that would not be denied. So, he wrote, "without too much regard for chronological order I shall range back and forth from the recollections of my childhood . . . to happenings of comparatively recent occurrence" (*EL,* 17).

He fulfilled his promise and found more than enough to write about. In his warm, friendly, leisurely, anecdotal fashion—a method admirably suited to this particular purpose—he rewrote and expanded material from his earlier *Myself—To Date* (1923), providing full and intimate accounts of his Paducah boyhood. The influence of Paducah and its people spring into focus. His apprentice newspaper years and his early experiences as a humorous writer and speaker come to life. He constructs illuminating vignettes of famous newspaper and magazine writers and editors he knew. He hosts the reader at the important events of the time.

Though the nation entered World War II at the end of the year in which the book appeared, *Exit Laughing* was and remained for two years an overwhelming success with the reading public. Critics and reviewers, some of whom had not always been kind to Cobb, were for the most part favorably impressed with this comprehensive, nearly six-hundred-page performance by a prolific and seasoned author who had seemed in danger of dropping out of sight.

One of the reviewers who could not enter honestly into the spirit of *Exit Laughing* was Robert Van Gelder of the *New York Times.* In Cobb's accounts of important people and events he caught something that seemed to him a tendency toward self-importance and name-dropping. To Van Gelder, Cobb emerges from the book "'with an enhanced chest expansion' that, to tell the truth, is still visible."[5]

But most others did not share this reaction. "The book gives a one-sided but fascinating picture of life in America from 1900 to about 1928," wrote one reviewer. "'Exit Laughing' is swift, easy, harmless entertainment."[6] Another concluded that it is "a lot of book. It rambles and is unconsciously wordy in spots, but it is friendly and human—genuine Cobb."[7] Reactions grow warmer and warmer, with comments that the book brings "something precious and lovable into American life and letters"[8] and "the implication of the title is that this will be his last literary effort. That would be a pity. The world never gets enough of its Twains and Rogerses and Cobbs."[9]

At a troubled time of his life, when he was plagued with illness and uncertain about his writing, the success of *Exit Laughing* was an immense satisfaction to Cobb. It was also an encouragement he needed almost desperately. But even as the signal triumph of his later years was being read and enjoyed widely under its lighthearted title, Cobb and his family were coming to grips with the undeniable recognition that the author would not be able to make his exit laughing. The funny fat man was slowly and painfully dying of dropsy.

The disease was long in its progress, with frequent remissions during which Cobb brightened and began to make plans for trips and holidays. But after these indeterminate periods, the symptoms always returned with increased force. Medically there was no cure for the condition, and the physician could concentrate only upon sustaining life as long as possible and upon keeping the patient comfortable. During remissions, Cobb welcomed friends like Leo Carrillo and Roland Young into his bedroom and sometimes kept them there most of the day and into the night. No man could have hoped for better comrades or more entertaining company.

By early summer of 1942 the disease had become seriously debilitating, and though Cobb tried manfully to remain optimistic, he had moments of depression. In July he wrote to an old friend in Kentucky, saying that he was "suffering from that incurable disease called getting old—and I've traded most of my emotions for symptoms.[10]

The family decided that things would be easier for all of them in New York, whereupon wife and daughter went ahead to arrange for a suite of rooms in a midtown hotel. They wrote letters back and forth prolifically, and by the time Irvin was to arrive by train, they expected to see him as they had left him. But at first they did not recognize him. "This bent old man, this slow-moving, shambling, thin old man?"[11] writes Elisabeth of this shocking moment.

He went to bed in the hotel suite, and in December 1943, rumors announced his death. So did the newspapers. But he immediately dispatched a humorous letter to the Associated Press, informing them that he would be sure to advise the newspapers "if I get ready to depart elsewhere."[12]

Shortly thereafter he secretly wrote one of the world's most remarkable letters. It was to be kept in the safe of Edwin J. Paxton, Sr., editor and publisher of the *Paducah Sun-Democrat,* and not to be opened until Cobb's death was officially confirmed. Cobb died in New York on 10 March 1944, and Paxton was the first to read the letter containing Cobb's explicit instructions regarding the disposal of his mortal remains. Paxton immediately sent copies of the letter to the press syndicates, and it was published all over the world.[13]

To large numbers of people, the letter seemed shocking in its rejection of most of the cherished traditions and religious ceremonies of burial. Having addressed it simply "To whom it may concern," Cobb requested that no person should see his face and that the family not wear "the bogus habiliments of so-called mourning." He wanted his body wrapped in a plain sheet and cremated in an "inexpensive container" without formal ceremonies. The ashes, also in a "plain container," were to be scattered among the roots of a newly planted dogwood tree in Oak Grove Cemetery at Paducah. The burial spot could be marked with a "slab of Kentucky limestone" or a "natural boulder of Southern granite," with only a bronze plate containing his name and the dates of his birth and death. (Elsewhere he had once written, "An epitaph on a tombstone is a belated advertisement for a line of goods that permanently has been discontinued.")[14]

Cobb wanted no show of grief, no "so-called Christian burial service" (which he called a "cruel and paganish" thing), but the pastor of the First Presbyterian Church could read the Twenty-Third Psalm. Cobb invited en masse his fellow members of the Elks Lodge and, by individual name, a large number of personal friends from Paducah. For the final requiem he would be "grateful if some of my colored friends sang, first 'Swing Low, Sweet Chariot' and then 'Deep River.'" To say a few words he suggested Tom Waller or one of two other Paducah friends. That was all.

Most of his wishes were respected. Initial services were held in New York on 13 March, when his family and all his close friends there (nearly sixty of them) paid tribute to him. But then some bizarre and heretofore little-known circumstances began to develop. According to his expressed wishes, the actual burial was to be in Paducah, but a series of unexpected events delayed the service for six months. Attorney Tom Waller[15] had composed the funeral address immediately and had timed it for eight minutes. But during the six months delay he had fretted over it and changed it so many times that he became doubtful whether he felt comfortable in delivering it. The service was eventually scheduled for 7 October 1944, whereupon the whole community geared up for an onrush of reporters and photographers from all over the country. On the day before the ceremonies, however, ex-presidential candidate Wendell Willkie died, and virtually all the news media diverted their coverage to that story. The Cobb ceremony went almost unnoticed outside of Kentucky.

Moreover, there was considerable trouble in following the explicit instructions Cobb had given. Because there is no "native stone" reasonably accessible in Kentucky, the "boulder" he requested was brought in from an entirely different region. A newly planted dogwood tree would not survive at that season; so the ashes could not be sprinkled over its roots. Instead, they were kept in a plain metal box that was to be lowered into a hole at the moment when Mr. Waller began his address. But it fell off the belt and caught sidewise in the hole, almost as though resisting the final pull of the grave. It had to be lowered unobtrusively after the ceremonies were over.[16]

Despite general expectations, Mr. Waller made no attempt to inject humor into his address, and it was eminently satisfactory for this highly sensitive occasion. Aside from the unforeseen difficulties, the ceremonies adhered scrupulously to Cobb's wishes.

The Joker in Spite of Himself

During Irvin Cobb's lifetime, honors of many kinds were heaped upon him. He was commissioned a major in the Intelligence Department of the Officers Reserve Corps of the United States Army. He was awarded the degree of Doctor of Laws by Dartmouth and the University of Georgia. He was a chevalier of the French Legion of Honor. His stories won many literary awards, and he has been the subject of more caricatures than has any other American writer.[17]

In 1922, ten leading literary figures voted by ballot to determine the respective merits of contemporary writers, and the results were nearly a clean sweep for Cobb. These men—eminent editors, critics, and writers—gave Cobb a unanimous first place as best writer of general humor, best all-around reporter, best local-colorist, best writer of horror tales, and best teller of anecdotes, in which he received both first and second places. This list was widely publicized at the time.[18]

As a writer, Cobb has been compared with a wide variety of other authors. Robert H. Davis, editor of *Munsey's Magazine,* contended that Cobb was a combination of Twain, Bret Harte, and Poe.[19] Some consider him America's greatest humorist since Twain and a better local-colorist than Harte.[20] Another declares that Cobb "displays the beauty, simplicity, and feeling of Harte and Stevenson; the flair for depicting the gruesome, the despair, and the terror of Poe; and the scintillating, unforced humor of Mark Twain and O. Henry at their best."[21] In fiction he has been called a descendant of Poe and Hawthorne.[22] As a humorist he has been most often compared with Twain; as a short-story local-colorist, with Bret Harte, Jack London, and O. Henry; and as a writer of horror tales, with Poe.[23] Don Marquis quipped, "Everything good that is said in New York is finally attributed to Irvin Cobb or Oliver Herford; and that is easy to understand, for they say more good things than anybody else."[24]

Shortly after Cobb's death, literary pundits began declaring his fiction out of date, and all of his works are now considered fallen into obscurity. Yet he has been widely praised for the universal qualities of his work and compared more than favorably with some of the popular but enduring writers in American literature. Cobb's essays and stories have been and continue to be reprinted in collections and anthologies. Moreover, in some unacknowledged way old Judge Priest survives with a tenacity that threatens to outlast all of us.

Apart from his place in the development of the horror story, however, Cobb seems destined to occupy a position of real importance as a humorist. Considering his extraordinary versatility, this judgment of history seems unfortunate. Cobb, who always regarded his humorous material as incidental to other things, would be profoundly disappointed. Of his sixty-odd books, fewer than half are primarily humorous.

Nonetheless, he appears to be securely entrenched as representing a necessary phase in the development of American humorous writing. In the first place, his sense of humor was nurtured in soil of a highly local composition. It was a kind of humor that was peculiar to western Kentucky, having qualities different not only from those of the general region but different also from those of the rest of Kentucky. This form of humor appears to be "a unique blend of humor, elegance, and traditional aristocracy that informs, deflates, corrects, and rebukes with courtesy and wit.[25] These distinctive qualities were always essential to Cobb's sense of humor, and they help to explain why people all over America recognized in it something unique and refreshing.

In a broader perspective, Cobb is of particular importance in "making use of all three type-figures in the humor of his time: the crackerbox sage, the solid citizen, and the Little Man.[26] His line of descent from humorist to humorist is suggested by Jean Shepherd, who contends that "the peculiar air of the Midwest . . . has molded most American humorists from Twain to Thurber by way of Cobb and Tarkington."[27] At any rate, despite his oft-expressed feelings to the contrary, Cobb seems at present to be remembered not as "the fat man with the enchanted pen"[28] but mostly as a Great American Funny Man.

One can always hope that the generally untested attitudes toward Cobb might change or at least broaden. For now it might be best and fairest all round to conclude with a speculation that seemed reasonable to Cobb. "Who knows what the end of anything is?" he asks at the end of *Exit Laughing*. "Who knows where a thing begins or when it may end?" (*EL*, 558).

In the broad view it appears that Cobb was, indeed, not merely funny. He was a very wise man.

Notes and References

Chapter One

1. Preface to *Back Home: Being the Narrative of Judge Priest and His People* (New York, 1912); hereafter cited in the text as *BH*.

2. "I Admit I Am a Good Reporter," *American Magazine* 88 (August 1919):60.

3. Fred G. Neuman, *Irvin S. Cobb, His Life and Letters* (Emaus, Pa., 1938), 192.

4. Ibid., 240.

5. Robert H. Davis, "Introducing Mr. Cobb," *Golden Book Magazine* 19 (January 1934):15a.

6. The interview was published in the *Paducah Sun-Democrat* and is recorded in Neuman's biography (258). In possibly its most dramatic form it is part of a longer quotation inscribed on a large brass plaque standing on Broadway in Paducah, across Third Street from Wallerstein's clothing store, on the side wall of which is painted a copy of a well known full-figure silhouette of Cobb, accompanied by the legend "Irvin S. Cobb bought his first suit at Wallerstein's."

7. This form of the quotation appears in Cobb's autobiography, *Exit Laughing* (New York, 1941), 75; hereafter cited in the text as *EL*. Among other places the clause "there never was but one Paducah" appears also as the last line of a widely read interview published by Alice Clark Kieft, "Man from Paducah," *Christian Science Monitor,* 13 May 1944, 6.

8. Inasmuch as historical investigations have found little evidence that a real Indian chief named Paduke ever existed, the stories about Paduke and his tribe might be considered purely legendary.

9. "Darkness," in *Sundry Accounts* (New York, 1922), 14.

10. See Cobb's "The Lost Tribes of the Irish in the South," *The World's Greatest Speeches,* ed. Lewis Copeland, 2d rev. ed. (New York, 1958), 722–729. In this address, which he delivered before the American Irish Historical Society in New York, 6 January 1917, Cobb expressed his pride in his Irish ancestry and contended that the combination of his Irish heritage and the Southern culture accounts for his creativity.

11. H. L. Mencken, "Heir of Mark Twain," in *Prejudices: First Series* (New York, 1919), 97–104.

12. *Myself—To Date* (New York, 1923), 15; hereafter cited in the text as *M*.

13. Elisabeth Cobb, *My Wayward Parent* (Indianapolis, 1945), 24.

14. Cobb's daughter "Buff" reveals that her father had felt a deep bit-

terness toward "Josh" Cobb until he began to wonder whether "Josh" had been trying to kill himself with liquor only for the sake of the family—so that they could collect his insurance. If so, says "Buff," the ploy worked, since the insurance was paid when "Josh" died four years after he began his steady drinking. See ibid., 24.

15. Ibid., 24–25.

16. Paducah had no public library until 1904. Therefore Cobb was heavily indebted to his grandfather Saunders and to "Uncle" Jo Shrewsbury for the development of his literary tastes beyond the standard classroom selections which he read at school.

17. Sara Smith Campbell, "Master of the Word," *Louisville Courier-Journal,* Sunday Magazine sec.; undated clipping in the Cobb collection at the Paducah Public Library. Mrs. Campbell was the wife of John Pearce Campbell, a distant cousin of Irvin Cobb. Mr. Campbell was still living in Paducah in 1975.

18. *A Plea for Old Cap Collier* (New York, 1921), 55.

19. Ibid., 54.

20. *All Aboard: Saga of the Romantic River* (New York, 1928), 2; hereafter cited in the text as *AA.* See also the following quotation from Donald Davidson, *The Tennessee,* vol. 2, *The New River: Civil War to TVA* (New York: Rinehart & Co., 1948), 285: "In its native son, Irvin S. Cobb, Paducah had produced the only eloquent literary spokesman of that tradition who had appeared on the Tennessee River. But the stories and sketches of his books were the swan song of the tradition, which was dying even as he wrote about it."

21. "Five Hundred Dollars Reward," in *Back Home,* 70.

22. "A Beautiful Evening," in *Old Judge Priest* (New York, 1916), 374.

23. Ibid., 392.

24. "Up Clay Street," in *Back Home,* 134.

25. *Kentucky* (New York, 1924), 38; hereafter cited in the text as *K.*

26. "A Blending of Parables," in *Old Judge Priest,* 56.

27. "The Lord Provides," in ibid., 16

28. See Twain's conclusion to *Tom Sawyer,* wherein he says, "So endeth this chronicle. It being strictly a history of a *boy,* it must stop here; the story could not go much further without becoming the history of a *man.*"

29. Booth Tarkington, *Penrod, His Complete Story* (New York, 1931), 583.

30. "Long Pants," in *Prose and Cons* (New York, 1926), 235; originally published as "The Long Pants Age," *Good Housekeeping,* August 1925, 30–32, 160, 163–64.

31. *Goin' on Fourteen* (New York, 1924), 218.

32. "The Advantage of Being Homely," in *Here Comes the Bride* (New York, 1925), 278–79.

33. "The Gossip Shop," *Bookman* 60 (January 1925):670.

34. "The Thrill of a Lifetime," in *Prose and Cons,* 293; originally pub-

lished as "The Greatest Thrill I Ever Had," *American Magazine* 90 (December 1920):54–55, 75–76.

35. "The Last of the Bourbons," in *Prose and Cons,* 209.

36. "A Dogged Underdog," in *Back Home,* 285.

37. Tom Waller, attorney at law, Paducah, Kentucky. During my interview with Mr. Waller in his Paducah law offices on 8 January 1975, he offered this interesting opinion concerning one of the reasons for Cobb's success as a writer. Only one month after the interview, Mr. Waller died in Paducah (8 February 1975).

38. John Wilson Townsend, *Irvin S. Cobb* (Atlanta, 1923), 160.

39. Alma E. Henderson, "Irvin S. Cobb," *American Author,* November 1932, 11.

40. "I Admit I am a Good Reporter," 290.

41. "How to Begin at the Top and Work Down," *American Magazine* 100 (August 1925):68.

42. From an interview by Pendennis: "'My Types'—Irvin S. Cobb," *Forum* 58 (October 1917):474.

Chapter Two

1. "Inside Stories," *Saturday Evening Post* 193 (10 July 1920):4.

2. In mentioning this column, Cobb's biographers and other writers have almost uniformly given the column heading in the following form: "Kentucky Sour Mash." Yet in my column-by-column examination of the *Louisville Evening Post* for the late spring and early summer of 1901, I find the heading to be invariably as I have described it and as I have cited it.

3. *Red Likker* (New York, 1929).

4. Quoted by Thomas L. Masson, *Our American Humorists* (New York, 1922), 97.

5. Though Cobb had intended "Sourmash" to be a regular daily feature, its appearance became highly irregular because Cobb was appointed political correspondent at about the same time he began writing the humorous column. As political correspondent, he frequently had to spend considerable time away from Louisville, especially when important political events were brewing in the capital city of Frankfort. Whenever he was gone from Louisville the "Sourmash" column was suspended without notice until he came back, whereupon the column appeared again, unannounced. There is no evidence that the column lost any of its readers through this cavalier management.

6. Quoted by Masson, *Our American Humorists,* 96.

7. Most of the really enterprising dailies appointed a special correspondent to cover important events in the state capital, and such a reporter was frequently distinguished by one of these titles. The terms are still in

common use today, though they may also be applied to radio and television correspondents.

8. Large portions of the account in *Exit Laughing* are taken from *Myself—To Date,* but some of it is altered slightly, and there is considerable fresh material as well.

9. "Big Moments of Big Trials, A Reporter's Story of Climaxes and Thrills," *McClure's* 46 (November 1915):90.

10. For several months after the shooting, Cobb was unaware that in the confusion of that momentous event he had been much closer to the action and far luckier than he knew. Seeing a wild-looking figure apparently in the act of fleeing across the capitol grounds in his shirt sleeves only moments after the shots were fired, a diligent policeman had come within a breath of shooting him down. For an intimate account of circumstances that attended Cobb's coverage of the trial, one should see Willard Rouse Jillson's *Irvin S. Cobb at Frankfort, Kentucky* (Carrollton, Ky., 1944), a scarce eight-page booklet. See the bibliography for this volume, which was published in three hundred copies.

11. Cobb appears to have been a compulsively conscientious courtroom reporter and sometimes an incredibly lucky one. He has told repeatedly of the time when he left town overnight during an adjournment and returned to find that a night session had been called in his absence. However, a friendly telegraph operator had sent to Louisville a copy of the official transcript—in Cobb's name. It turned out to be a far better account than anything sent in by Cobb's rivals. Cobb tells the story separately in "Trial and Error," *Readers' Digest* 41 (December 1942):32.

12. The main substance of this paragraph is from Elisabeth Cobb, *My Wayward Parent,* 26–27.

13. During my brief but memorable interview with Harriet Boswell, retired librarian of the Carnegie Public Library in Paducah, she talked familiarly and charmingly of the Thornbury girls and their family, and she gave me a picture of the Thornbury house as it must have appeared when the girls were of college age. Like many Paducahans, Miss Boswell is very proud of Irvin Cobb. To the oldtimers, he is still just a home-town boy whose success in the outside world is both gratifying and perplexing.

14. Ernest Hemingway, (New York: Viking Press, 1958), quoted by Charles A. Fenton, *The Apprenticeship of Ernest Hemingway* 161. By the middle of his career as a writer of fiction, Cobb may have reached a similar conclusion about the adverse effects of an overlong career in journalism. See for example the opening paragraphs of *Murder Day by Day* (Indianapolis, 1933). Here Cobb conveniently makes his central character an old-line newsman and newspaper editor who says to the reader "The newspaper trade is a good trade to climb by . . . it's a poor trade to stick by for long" (13).

15. Neuman, *Irvin S. Cobb,* 63.

16. Robert H. Davis, *Irvin S. Cobb, Storyteller* (New York, n.d.), 11.

17. Elisabeth Cobb, *My Wayward Parent,* 67–68.

18. In later references to the episode, Cobb retains the tone of this letter, as he does in this typical comment: "I had come to New York with a view to revolutionizing metropolitan journalism, and journalism had shown a reluctance amounting to positive diffidence about coming forward and being revolutionized" (*Cobb's Bill-of-Fare* [New York, 1913], 72).

19. This shrewd but affable editor was the regular city editor, Tommy Dieuaide, who had taken over the post as managing editor only as a substitute, to work that particular shift for that day. This arrangement seems to have been a common occurrence on the *Sun* in those years. In later years, Cobb invariably spoke of Tommy Dieuaide with warmth and respect.

20. "Inside Stories," 4.

21. Ibid., 147.

22. Sloane Gordon, "The Story of Irvin S. Cobb," *Pearson's Magazine,* 33 (March 1915):279.

23. Townsend, *Irvin S. Cobb,* 160.

24. Davis, *Irvin S. Cobb, Storyteller,* 11.

25. *Newsweek,* 20 March 1944, 98. In his coverage of the sensational Thaw trial, Cobb distinguished himself for his capacity to seize upon the perfectly apt detail and upon the illuminating turn of phrase in the testimony. As one might expect, Cobb took full advantage of the bizarre aspects of the case, and for those readers who wanted to follow the trial by means of newspaper accounts, no other correspondent provided so complete and so vivid a record of the moment-by-moment developments in the courtroom. To get an adequate idea of Cobb's attitude toward the whole affair and of his treatment of it, see the detailed account in *Exit Laughing* (228–48) and the article "Big Moments of Big Trials" already cited here (note 9). One might profitably consult the following accounts also: "A Woman Tells," in *Star Reporters and 34 of Their Stories,* ed. Louis Leo Snyder and Richard Brandon Norris (New York, 1949): "Irvin S. Cobb writes 600,000 Words on the Harry K. Thaw Murder Trial—Sensation of the Pre-Kinseyan Era," *New York Sun,* 26 June 1906; and "You Have Ruined My Wife!" *New York Evening World,* 7 February 1907.

26. "The Great Reduction," *Saturday Evening Post* 194 (16 July 1921):4.

27. Ellis Parker Butler, "Mr. Cobb of Paducah," in *Obiter Dictum;* reprinted in *Who's Cobb and Why?* (Louisville, Ky., n.d.), 12.

28. *Compositions of a Newspaper Minion* is the subtitle Cobb provided for his book *Stickfuls* (New York, 1923). Cobb changed *Stickfuls* to *Myself—To Date* after the book had been on the market for only a short time, and with the new title he dropped the subtitle. *Myself—To Date* has no subtitle.

29. Helen Bullitt Lowry, "If You Have Talent," *Good Housekeeping* 80 (February 1925):43.

30. "The Wasted Headline," *Saturday Evening Post* 192 (8 May 1920):10.

31. Interview by Robert Van Gelder, in *Writers and Writing* (New York, 1946), 236.

Chapter Three

1. Masson, *Our American Humorists,* 99–100.
2. Elisabeth Cobb, *My Wayward Parent,* 97.
3. Norris W. Yates, "The Cracker-Barrel Sage in the West and South: Will Rogers and Irvin S. Cobb," in *The American Humorist: Conscience of the Twentieth Century* (Ames, Iowa, 1964), 131.
4. "Irvin S. Cobb Proves That Humorists Are Able to Buy Food," *Literary Digest* 62 (19 July 1919):58.
5. Sara Smith Campbell, "The Clown Prince of Gourmets," *Louisville Courier-Journal,* Sunday Magazine sec., undated.
6. Norris W. Yates, *Robert Benchley* (New York: Twayne, 1968), 136. Like Benchley, Cobb was a bumbler with machinery. See Elisabeth Cobb, *My Wayward Parent,* 107–8: "If forced to employ any tool of any description, there was going to be an accident. He could get a nutpick out of order. Arm him with tools, gadgets, can openers, ropes, shovels, any mechanical devices or dull blunt instruments, and before he was done he would not only have managed to scar himself all up—but also all and sundry who dared approach within twenty feet of him."
7. Though H. L. Mencken wrote "The Heir of Mark Twain" to argue that "Speaking of Operations—" is merely a collection of old wheezes, even Mencken admits the aptness, felicity, and originality of this phrase.
8. Beginning as a magazine article titled "Life Among the Abandoned Farmers," this humorous essay was included in *Those Times and These* in 1917. Then it was expanded to a full-sized book titled *The Abandoned Farmers* in 1920.
9. "Travel," in *"Here Comes the Bride"* (New York, 1925), 218–53.
10. Mark Twain, *The Innocents Abroad,* vol. 1 (New York: Harper & Brothers, 1911), preface.
11. *Europe Revised* (New York, 1914), 19–20.
12. Masson, *Our American Humorists,* 102–3.
13. "He'd Be 100 Today," *Paducah Sun-Democrat,* 23 June 1976.

Chapter Four

1. "The Trail of the Lonesome Laugh," *Everybody's Magazine* 24 (April 1911); later adapted as chapter 8 of *Myself—To Date.*
2. "Censorship or Not," *Literary Digest* 27 (23 June 1923):29.
3. Quoted by Edward Angly, "What's the Matter With the United States?" *New York Herald,* 8 May 1932, 20.
4. "Politics on the Cobb," *Nation* (17 July 1920):62.
5. E. J. Kahn, Jr., *The World of Swope* (New York, 1965), 166–67.

6. C. G. Paulding, "On All Fours," *Commonweal* 39 (24 December 1943):245.

7. Henry L. Stuart, "Irvin S. Cobb," *Book News Monthly,* February 1914, 270. One of Cobb's perennial favorites among the topical essays is "A Plea for Old Cap Collier," but since this essay has been discussed in chapter 1, it will not be considered again in this chapter.

8. Few of the Algonquin Wits themselves could "crack wise" more spontaneously or more effectively than could Cobb. A widely repeated anecdote is the best case in point. One of the leading Wits was Franklin P. Adams (F. P. A.), whose square-topped head and long-nosed, long-lipped face was much caricatured. Upon entering the Algonquin Hotel one day, Cobb saw that the lobby displayed conspicuously a new conversation piece—a stuffed moose head. Cobb halted in mock horror and threw out both arms, bringing his luncheon companions to a sudden stop. "My God!" said Cobb, "somebody has shot Frank Adams!" For one version of this story, see Corey Ford, *The Time of Laughter* (Boston: Little, Brown & Co., 1967), 13.

9. Actually, Cobb and Rinehart were close friends at the time when they perpetrated this mock-literary warfare. As prominent members of the "Lorimer school of fiction," they had been warm friends for several years, and as writers they enjoyed a mutual respect. They considered this literary hoax great fun. See John Tebbel, *George Horace Lorimer and The Saturday Evening Post* (New York: Doubleday & Co., 1948), 62–64.

10. Selection 26, however, is a short story called "The Gold Brick Twins." Like many other "orphans" in Cobb's anthologies, it does not really belong in this collection.

11. Whether or not Cobb was aware of the fact, the "bore" was a ubiquitous topic in the literary form known as the character sketch, or merely the "character," which goes all the way back to Theophrastus in the second century B.C. "The Bore" is also the title of one of Horace's most widely read "Characters" in verse. Actually Horace (65–8 B.C.) considered this poem a form of satire.

12. "Unaccustomed As I Am—" can be found in *Prose and Cons,* 258–78.

13. I have altered the original order of selections so that I can present here the two childhood essays in logical sequence. This collection offers a good illustration of Cobb's penchant for printing his previously published stories and essays in altogether random sequences. In *Prose and Cons,* for instance, "Unaccustomed As I Am—" separates the two essays of childhood reminiscence.

14. Even though the four humorous essays in *Both Sides of the Street* are the last which Cobb published in book form, in 1940 the Sun Dial Press issued a typically miscellaneous collection of Cobb's work under the title of *Irvin Cobb at His Best.* Four of these are humorous essays that we have already discussed. Another such essay, "The Young Nuts of America," is actually the

first section of Cobb's humorous novel *Fibble, D.D.* (New York, 1916). The remaining selection, "The Life of the Party," is humorous fiction. All were originally published between 1915 and 1923.

15. See, for instance, p. 308, where Cobb makes a sly comment upon "literary" style: "Come we now—that's the way the fancy writers like to put it—come we now to the really tragic figure of the three. . . ."

16. I draw this inference from remarks several librarians have made to me during my research.

17. Fred Lewis Pattee, *The New American Literature, 1890–1930* (New York, 1968), 325.

18. Ibid., 324.

19. Quoted in "American Humorists—Irvin S. Cobb," *Journal of the National Educational Association* 14 (March 1925):101.

20. "American Readers Will Miss Them," *Senior Scholastic* 44 (1 May 1944):22.

21. Interview by Pendennis, "'My Types'—Irvin S. Cobb," 476.

22. See Townsend, *Irvin S. Cobb,* 165.

23. Grant Overton, "Irvin S. Cobb: Ask Him Another," *Bookman* 65 (August 1927):674.

24. Elisabeth Cobb, *My Wayward Parent,* 106.

25. Arnold Bennett, *Your United States: Impressions of a First Visit* (New York, 1912), 148.

26. "The Trail of the Lonesome Laugh," in *Myself—To Date,* 338–39.

27. Overton, "Irvin S. Cobb: Ask Him Another," 675.

28. E. V. Lucas, quoted by Wade Hall, *The Smiling Phoenix: Southern Humor from 1865 to 1914* (Gainsville, Fla., 1965), 314.

29. "Life on the Bounding Red Ink," in *Prose and Cons,* 298.

30. Elisabeth Cobb, *My Wayward Parent,* 135–36.

31. Ibid., 155–56.

32. Interview with Alice Clark Kieft, "Man from Paducah," *Christian Science Monitor,* 13 May 1944, 6.

33. See the account of this episode by John Tebbel, *The Compact History of the American Newspaper* (New York, 1963), 215.

34. Irvin Cobb to Thomas B. Costain, 23 May 1941, Irvin S. Cobb collection in the University of Kentucky Library.

35. See William Rose Benét, "Mortality in Writers," *Saturday Review of Literature* 27 (18 March 1944):14.

36. Frederick G. Melcher, "Three Good Men," *Publisher's Weekly,* 18 March 1944, 1201.

37. "How to Begin at the Top and Work Down," 70.

38. Ibid.

39. Ibid., 34.

40. Ibid., 70.

41. In his late years, Ernest Hemingway was a conspicuous example of

the significant writer who strenuously avoids talking about his current work lest he might talk away its "juice" (Hemingway to Wayne Chatterton, in conversation at Ketchum, Idaho, 1958).

42. See Gordon, "The Story of Irvin S. Cobb," 281: "When he gets an idea for a story or a series, he talks it over and over with his friends and gets their viewpoint."

43. A letter from Cobb to one Paul Bunn of St. Louis, dated only "Nov. 27." Though the letter does not give the year of composition, and though the content indicates that it was probably written several years after Cobb wrote his first humorous stories, his attitude toward the evolution of contemporary taste indicates that he had been aware of these tendencies for a considerable time. Cobb's observations upon humorous fiction help at least partially to explain his acceptance of the charge to discover whether he could write fiction for the "SatEvePost," where good fiction enjoyed a high priority in pay and popularity.

44. *World's Great Humorous Stories,* ed. Cobb (Cleveland, 1944), 12.

45. Ibid. 14.

46. Ibid.

47. Some of his novels contain broad farcical elements, however, particularly *J. Poindexter* and *Fibble, D.D.*

48. *The Life of the Party* (New York, 1919).

49. *From Place to Place* (New York, 1920), 342–407.

50. *"Here Comes the Bride,"* 303–40.

51. *Ladies and Gentlemen* (New York, 1927), 28–66.

52. *Snake Doctor,* (New York, 1923), 142–78.

53. *This Man's World* (New York, 1929), 153–63; hereafter cited in the text as *TM.*

54. *On an Island That Cost $24.00* (New York, 1926), 114–43.

55. *One Way to Stop a Panic* (New York, 1933), 17–59.

56. *The Escape of Mr. Trimm* (New York, 1913), 202–41; hereafter cited in the text as *E;* also published separately by Doran in 1918, and included in *From Place to Place,* 55–95.

57. *The Thunders of Silence* (New York, 1918), 27.

58. The quotations from Fisher are taken from his essay "How's Your Sense of Humor?" in *The Neurotic Nightingale* (Milwaukee: Casanova Press, 1935), 29–30.

59. Cyril Clemens, "A Chat with Irvin S. Cobb," *Hobbies* 49 (August 1944):100–101.

60. Benét, "Mortality in Writers," 14.

61. Rollin Lynde Hartt, "Irvin S. Cobb Proves That Humorists Are Able to Buy Food," *Literary Digest* 62 (19 July 1919):58–60.

62. Overton, "Irvin S. Cobb: Ask Him Another," 674.

63. Overton, "Cobb's Fourth Dimension," in *When Winter Comes to Main Street* (New York, 1922), 179.

64. Will Rogers in the postscript to Cobb's *Piano Jim and the Impotent Pumpkin Vine, or Charley Russell's Best Story—To My Way of Thinking* (Lexington, Ky.: Bluegrass Bookshop, 1950), 25.

65. Masson tells this version of the story in *Our American Humorists*, 93.

Chapter Five

1. "Exit Laughing," *Newsweek*, 20 March 1944, 98.

2. The exact number of Old Judge Priest stories has been a matter of wide and variant speculation. In the *Newsweek* article previously cited, the number is set at one hundred stories "all told," though no evidence is offered to support this declaration. Neuman's biography places the number at forty-six (98), but for some reason which I fail to understand, Neuman insists upon including at least two stories that appear to be exclusively about Judge Priest's black servant, Jeff Poindexter. I prefer to consider the Jeff Poindexter stories more legitimately as contributions to Cobb's tales about the black people. If one accepts this classification, the number of Judge Priest stories that were published in book form is forty-four, including the two short novels that comprise *Judge Priest Turns Detective*.

3. Some fiction writers who appear to be exceptions are not really exceptions at all. For instance, after twenty years as a successful reporter and editor, A. B. Guthrie, Jr., wrote some excellent novels, one of which, *The Way West*, brought him the Pulitzer Prize. But in his autobiography, *The Blue Hen's Chick*, Guthrie provides an account of the grueling retraining that he had to impose upon himself before he was able to produce his first important piece of fiction (see 168–81).

4. Pendennis, "'My Types'—Irvin S. Cobb," 475.

5. Thomas S. "Tom" Waller, attorney at law. Mr. Waller made this comment during my interview with him at his Paducah office on 8 January 1975.

6. Pendennis, "'My Types'—Irvin S. Cobb," 471.

7. Kathleen H. Henderson, "Judge William Sutton Bishop," *Advance-Yeoman* (Wyckliffe, Ky.), 7 September 1972, 3.

8. Quoted by Sloane Gordon, "The Story of Irvin S. Cobb," 279.

9. This was the phrase which Cobb's distant cousin John Pearce Campbell used during my interview with him in 1975. Apparently many Paducahns of Cobb's generation called Connie Lee a "foot doctor" instead of the more "'highfalutin'" word *chiropodist*. Cobb, however, uses the latter term in writing about Connie Lee.

10. *Glory, Glory Hallelujah!* (Indianapolis, 1941), 11.

11. This date is supplied by Sara Smith Campbell in an undated article titled "Master of the Word." Though the article probably appeared in one of the Louisville newspapers, the only clipping to which I have had access does not indicate the source of the article nor the page numbers. The clipping can

be found in the Cobb collection at the Paducah Public Library. At any rate, Connie Lee outlived all the other Paducah people upon whom Cobb based his fictional characters, and by more than a decade Lee outlived the author himself.

12. Neuman gives the middle initial of Dr. Brooks as *B* instead of *G* (*Irvin S. Cobb*, 91). The full middle name of Dr. Brooks was Gaunt.

13. Irvin Cobb to Herbert Wallerstein, 5 January 1943, Santa Monica, California. Herbert Wallerstein included the letter in a small booklet titled *Cobbiana*, which appeared in January 1947. See note 15.

14. From my interview with Tom Waller.

15. On 8 January 1975—also the day of my interview with attorney Thomas Waller—I talked with Herbert ("Herb") Wallerstein for nearly two hours in Wallerstein's clothing store in Paducah, where Mr. Wallerstein still worked for a few hours every business day. According to Mr. Wallerstein, the main physical characteristics of the store have not changed greatly since Irvin Cobb's boyhood days. In 1975 it was still one of Paducah's best downtown clothing stores, and the community seemed to realize that it was one of the last places of business that survived from the days when Cobb was a resident. "Herb" Wallerstein, who had known him from Wallerstein's childhood days, seemed pleased with Cobb's fictional treatments of the elder Wallerstein. Alert and quick-witted despite long illness and advancing age, Mr. Wallerstein cultivated a mischievous cynicism that failed to conceal the fact that he almost idolized Irvin Cobb. Indeed, "Herb" once spent considerable time and effort in an unsuccessful attempt to convince the United States Postal Service to issue an Irvin S. Cobb commemorative stamp.

16. The ensuing references to some of Cobb's black characters and their real-life counterparts can be found in *Glory, Glory Hallelujah!*, 11–29.

17. Elisabeth Cobb, *My Wayward Parent*, 109.

18. Ibid., 111.

19. James Playsted Wood, *The Curtis Magazines* (New York, 1971), 104.

20. Tebbel, *George Horace Lorimer and The Saturday Evening Post*, 63.

21. Ibid., 64.

22. The publishing firm for this volume was known simply as Ray Long and Richard R. Smith, Inc., New York.

23. In the first Judge Priest story, "Words and Music," for instance, the old Judge has to testify under oath in a courtroom. As part of the examination, he has to disclose the place and date of his birth (Calloway County, Kentucky, 27 July 1839). He also testifies that he was first admitted to the bar in 1865, that he has held his judicial post for sixteen years, and that from the date of his admission to the bar all the way to the time of this testimony he has served continuously in that position. For four years between April of 1861 and June of 1865 he had served in "the war for the Southern Confederacy" (24). Another example of this kind of information is that, much later, in "April Fool" (*Down*

Yonder with Judge Priest and Irvin S. Cobb [New York, 1932],; hereafter cited in the text as *DY.*), the old Judge's age is given as seventy.

24. "The Sun Shines Bright," in *Down Yonder*, 27.

25. This masterpiece of eerie fiction is "An Occurrence up a Side-Street," a worthy companion to Cobb's earlier success in a similar vein, "The Escape of Mr. Trimm."

26. "Forrest's Last Charge," in *Old Judge Priest* (New York, 1916), 308; hereafter cited in the text as *OJ.*

27. "An Incident of the Noble Experiment," in *Down Yonder*, 271.

28. At one place in the Judge Priest stories the narrator mentions rather off-handedly a "rusty Ford" that Jeff sometimes drove after the old horse died. But this is the only reference to this vehicle. It plays no important part in the Judge Priest series.

29. "Ole Miss," in *Down Yonder*, 260.

30. "Judge Priest Comes Back," in *Old Judge Priest*, 11–112.

31. "According to the Code," in ibid., 232–76, and "Br'er Fox and the Brier Patch," in *Down Yonder*, 109–24.

32. See *Judge Priest Turns Detective*, (Indianapolis, 1937), 16 and passim; hereafter cited in the text as *JP.*

33. "An Incident of the Noble Experiment," in *Down Yonder*, 273.

34. "Great Day in the Morning," in ibid., 85–108.

35. "Double-Barrelled Justice," in *Old Judge Priest*, 355.

36. "Uncle Sam Collaborating," in *Down Yonder*, 203–22.

37. *Down Yonder with Judge Priest and Irvin S. Cobb* (1932).

38. See *Judge Priest Turns Detective*, 11–13.

39. "The Cater-Cornered Sex," in *Sundry Accounts* (New York, 1922), 57–103.

40. "A Colonel of Kentucky," in *Down Yonder*, 170–202.

41. "Up Clay Street," in *Back Home*, 131–66.

42. "The Good Lord Provides," in *Old Judge Priest*, 11–48.

43. "The Sun Shines Bright," in *Down Yonder*, 32.

44. "The County Trot," in *Back Home*, 3–36.

45. "When the Fighting Was Good," in ibid., 167–200.

46. "A Blending of the Parables," in *Old Judge Priest*, 49–91.

47. "April Fool," in *Down Yonder*, 13.

48. "The Cure for Lonesomeness," in *Those Times and These* (New York, 1917), 138–68.

49. "Hark! From the Tombs," in ibid., 218–57.

50. *J. Poindexter, Col.* (New York, 1922).

51. "The Sun Shines Bright," in *Down Yonder*, 40–41.

52. This was "Under Sentence," a collaborative effort with Roi Cooper Megrue. See Townsend, *Irvin S. Cobb*, 163.

53. "Fox Has Smash Hit with Rogers in 'Judge Priest,'" *Hollywood Reporter*, 4 August 1934, 3.

54. "Irvin S. Cobb: He'd Be 100 Today," *Paducah Sun-Democrat*, 23 June 1976, 4–A.

55. "Down in Old Kentucky," *Christian Science Monitor*, 23 May 1932, 5.

Chapter Six

1. This unpublished letter is in the Cobb collection at the University of Kentucky. It is one of four original handwritten letters sent to the university from the offices of Doubleday & Co., Inc., New York, at the request of Mr. Lawrence S. Thompson, who was then director of libraries at the university. Mr. Costain was then an editor at Doubleday.

2. In the cover letter (7 February 1951) that accompanied the four Cobb letters mentioned in note 1, Ethel M. Hulse of Doubleday, Doran, wrote, "The project was never carried out."

3. *Cobb's Cavalcade* (Cleveland, 1945), 125–260.

4. B. D. Zevin, in ibid., 12.

5. Here was the "funny fat man," no longer with new excursions into humor, but with a gripping short story about a man enduring almost superhuman adversities.

6. In Masson, *Our American Humorists*, 101.

7. Stuart, "Irvin S. Cobb," 270.

8. Henderson, "Irvin S. Cobb," 11.

9. See Arthur Bartlett Maurice, "The History of Their Books," *Bookman* 69 (July 1929):104.

10. Besides the previously cited "My Story That I Like Best," see also, among other accounts, Cobb's *Exit Laughing*, 332 ff.; his contribution to *My Maiden Effort*, published for the Author's League of America (Garden City, N.Y., 1921), 40–42; Pendennis, "'My Types'—Irvin S. Cobb," 473; and Maurice, "The History of Their Books," 511.

11. Maurice, "The History of their Books," 511.

12. "My Maiden Effort," 42.

13. *Local Color* (New York, 1916), 204–43.

14. Maurice, "The History of Their Books," 513–14.

15. *Sundry Accounts*, 11–56.

16. *Local Color*, 129–59.

17. *Snake Doctor*, 11–48.

18. See *First Prize Stories, 1919–1960* (Garden City, N.Y., 1960), 51–68.

19. *Faith, Hope and Charity* (Cleveland, 1942), 129–52.

20. *Ladies and Gentlemen*, 202–25.

21. *From Place to Place*, 156–205.

22. *Faith, Hope and Charity*, 11–38.

23. Overton, *When Winter Comes to Main Street*, 176.

24. Gordon, "The Story of Irvin S. Cobb," 278. Even among Cobb's close friends and acquaintances were some discriminating readers who could see little in "The Belled Buzzard." Tom Waller, for instance, whom Cobb personally selected to read the eulogy at his funeral, was outspoken about this matter. "I could never see much in 'The Belled Buzzard,'" he said, "but I am impressed by some of the others." See my interview with Waller.

Chapter Seven

1. An anecdote helps to illustrate the extent to which Cobb was immediately associated with Kentucky whiskey in the minds of Southerners: In a letter dated 10 October 1933 from the Players Club in New York, Henry W. Lanier, son of the eminent Southern poet Sidney Lanier, wrote to Cobb, "Can the author of the Coming of Whiskey to Kentucky help the Players to get at a proper price a barrel of really fine rye, which we could bottle here with the Players label—as we did in ancient days? Uncut, unblended and undefiled rye!" On 20 October, in response to Lanier's request, Cobb forwarded the letter to an old friend in Lexington, asking that the whiskey be sent directly to the Players Club. Both letters are in the Cobb collection at the University of Kentucky.

2. Andres Österling, secretary of the Nobel Prize Committee, in the Nobel Prize citation to Hemingway in 1954. This is the phrasing used by Carlos Baker in the "authorized" biography of Hemingway, *Ernest Hemingway: A Life Story* (New York: Charles Scribner's Sons, 1969), 528.

3. Elisabeth Cobb, *My Wayward Parent,* 175.

4. Ibid., 181.

5. Robert Van Gelder, "The Latest Biography by Irvin S. Cobb.," *New York Times Book Review,* 16 November 1941, 4.

6. George Joel, "Irvin Cobb's World," *Nation* 5 (17 May 1941):570.

7. Stanley Walker, "Mellow and Friendly as His Native Bourbon," *New York Herald-Tribune Books,* 16 March 1941, 1.

8. William Allen White, "The Humor of the Self-Kidder," *Saturday Review of Literature* 23 (22 March 1941):5.

9. M. W. B., "The Bookshelf, Accent on the Laugh," *Christian Science Monitor,* 1 April 1941, 18.

10. Cobb to John Wilson Townsend, 3 July 1942; this letter is in the Cobb collection at the University of Kentucky.

11. Elisabeth Cobb, *My Wayward Parent,* 246.

12. *Newsweek,* 20 December 1943, 70.

13. Copies of this letter can be found in many places. For most people, the easiest place to find a copy is probably in Elisabeth Cobb's *My Wayward Parent,* 249–55. My references to, paraphrasing of, and excerpts from the letter are from this source.

14. Quoted by B. D. Zevin, in *Cobb's Cavalcade,* 11.

15. This information on the Paducah services is from my interview with Thomas Waller.

16. Inasmuch as Mr. Waller died shortly after my interview with him, I can relate a story that he did not wish told publicly until he had passed away. Immediately after Cobb's funeral services, a woman inquired of Mr. Waller whether Mr. Cobb's head was to the East. Mr. Waller reminded her that in his present form Mr. Cobb had no head.

17. See the long list of artists and illustrators who have made one or more caricatures of Cobb, in Neuman's *Irvin S. Cobb,* p. 239.

18. Robert H. Davis, editor of *Munsey's,* first made these results public in the *New York Herald,* 23 April 1922. It can be found reprinted in Grant Overton's *When Winter Comes to Main Street,* 183–84.

19. Gordon, "The Story of Irvin S. Cobb," 284.

20. Piercy, *Modern Writers at Work,* 646.

21. Henderson, "Irvin S. Cobb," 11.

22. Stuart, "Irvin S. Cobb," 270.

23. Townsend, *Irvin S. Cobb,* 165.

24. Don Marquis, "Confessions of a Reformed Columnist," *Saturday Evening Post* 201 (29 December 1928):59.

25. Henderson, "Judge William Sutton Bishop," 1.

26. Yates, *The American Humorist,* 129.

27. Jean Shepherd, introduction to *The America of George Ade* (New York: G. P. Putnam's Sons, 1962), 10.

28. "A Humorist and His Wrist-Watch," *Literary Digest* 53 (12 August 1916):378.

Selected Bibliography

PRIMARY SOURCES

1. Books

The Abandoned Farmers. New York: George H. Doran Co., 1920.

Alias Ben Alibi. New York: George H. Doran Co., 1925.

All Aboard; Saga of the Romantic River. New York: Cosmopolitan, 1928.

Azam; the Story of An Arabian Colt and His Friends. Chicago: Rand, McNally & Co., 1937.

Back Home: Being the Narrative of Judge Priest and His People. New York: George H. Doran Co., 1912.

Both Sides of the Street. New York: Cosmopolitan, 1930.

Chivalry Peak. New York: Cosmopolitan, 1927.

Cobb's Anatomy. New York: George H. Doran Co., 1912.

Cobb's Bill-of-Fare. New York: George H. Doran Co., 1913.

Cobb's Cavalcade: A Selection of the Writings of Irvin S. Cobb. Edited, with introduction, by B. D. Zevin. Cleveland: World Publishing Co., 1945.

Down Yonder with Judge Priest and Irvin S. Cobb. New York: R. Long & R. R. Smith, 1932.

Eating in Two or Three Languages. New York: George H. Doran Co., 1919.

The Escape of Mr. Trimm: His Plight and Other Plights. New York: George H. Doran Co., 1913.

Europe Revised. New York: George H. Doran Co., 1914.

Exit Laughing. Indianapolis: Bobbs-Merrill Co.

Faith, Hope and Charity. Cleveland: World Publishing Co., 1942.

Favorite Humorous Stories of Irvin S. Cobb. New York: Triangle Books, 1940.

Fibble D. D. New York: George H. Doran Co., 1916.

From Place to Place. New York: George H. Doran Co., 1920.

The Glory of the Coming: What Mine Eyes Have Seen of Americans in Action in This Year of Grace and Allied Endeavor. New York: George H. Doran Co., 1918.

Goin' on Fourteen: Being Cross-sections Out of a Year in the Life of an Average Boy. New York: George H. Doran Co., 1924.

The Governors of Kentucky. Lexington, Ky.: Bluegrass Bookshop, 1947.

"Here Comes the Bride—," and So Forth. New York: George H. Doran Co., 1925.

Incredible Truth. New York: Cosmopolitan, 1931.

Indiana. New York: George H. Doran Co., 1924.

Irvin Cobb at His Best. Garden City, N.Y.: Sun Dial Press, 1923; Garden City, N.Y.: Doubleday, Doran & Co., 1929; Sun Dial Press, 1936, 1940.

J. Poindexter, Colored. New York: George H. Doran Co., 1922.

Judge Priest Turns Detective. Indianapolis: Bobbs-Merrill Co., 1937.

Kansas. George H. Doran Co., 1924.

Kentucky. New York: George H. Doran Co., 1924.

Ladies and Gentlemen. New York: Cosmopolitan, 1927; Freeport, N.Y.: Books for Libraries Press, 1970.

A Laugh A Day Keeps the Doctor Away: His Favorite Stories as Told by Irvin S. Cobb. New York: George H. Doran Co., 1923.

The Life of the Party. New York: George H. Doran Co., 1919.

Local Color. New York: George H. Doran Co., 1916.

Maine. New York: George H. Doran Co., 1924.

Many Laughs for Many Days: Another Year's Supply of His Favorite Stories as Told by Irvin S. Cobb. New York: George H. Doran Co., 1925; Garden City, N.Y.: Garden City Publishing Co., 1925, 1933.

Murder Day by Day. Indianapolis: Bobbs-Merrill Co., 1933.

Myself—To Date. New York: Review of Reviews, 1923. Earlier published under title *Stickfuls.*

New York. George H. Doran Co., 1924.

North Carolina. New York: George H. Doran Co., 1924.

"Oh, Well, You Know How Women Are!" New York: George H. Doran Co., 1920.

Old Judge Priest. New York: George H. Doran Co., 1916; Grosset & Dunlap, 1916.

On an Island That Cost $24.00. New York: George H. Doran Co., 1926.

One Third Off. New York: George H. Doran Co., 1921.

One Way to Stop a Panic. New York: R. M. McBride & Co., 1933.

Paths of Glory: Impressions of War Written at and Near the Front. New York: George H. Doran Co., 1915.

Piano Jim and the Impotent Pumpkin Vine. Lexington, Ky.: Bluegrass Bookshop, 1950.

A Plea for Old Cap Collier. New York: George H. Doran Co., 1921.

Prose and Cons. New York: George H. Doran Co., 1926.

Red Likker. New York: Cosmopolitan, 1929.

Roll Call. Indianapolis: Bobbs-Merrill Co., 1942.

Roughing It Deluxe. New York: George H. Doran Co., 1914.

Snake Doctor and Other Stories. New York: George H. Doran Co., 1923.

Some United States: A Series of Stops in Various Parts of This Nation with One Excursion Across the Line. New York: George H. Doran Co., 1926.

Speaking of Operations. New York: George H. Doran Co., 1915.

Speaking of Prussians. New York: George H. Doran Co., 1917.
Stickfuls: Compositions of a Newspaper Minion. New York: George H. Doran Co.,
    1923. Also published under title *Myself—To Date.*
Sundry Accounts. New York: George H. Doran Co., 1922.
This Man's World. New York: Cosmopolitan, 1929.
Those Times and These. New York: George H. Doran Co., 1917.
The Thunders of Silence. New York: George H. Doran Co., 1918.
To Be Taken Before Sailing. New York: Cosmopolitan, 1930.
"Who's Who" Plus "Here's How!" New York: Hotel Waldorf-Astoria, 1934.
The Works of Irvin S. Cobb. 4 vols. New York: Review of Reviews, 1912–20.
The Works of Irvin S. Cobb. 10 vols. George H. Doran Co., 1912–20.

2. Edited Books
The World's Great Humorous Stories. Cleveland: World Publishing Co., 1944.

3. Articles, Speeches, and Stories in Anthologies and Collections
"The Belled Buzzard." In *Golden Tales of the Old South,* edited by May Lam-
    berton Becker. New York: Dodd, Mead, & Co., 1930.
"Boys Will Be Boys." In *The Best Short Stories of 1917 and Yearbook of the
    American Short Story,* edited by Edward J. O'Brien. Boston: Small, May-
    nard & Co., 1918. Also in *The Best of the Best American Short Stories 1915–
    1950,* edited by Martha Foley. Boston: Houghton-Mifflin Co., 1952.
"The Chocolate Hyena." In *The Best Short Stories of 1923 and Yearbook of the
    American Short Story,* edited by J. O'Brien. Boston: Small, Maynard &
    Co., 1924.
"A Colonel of Kentucky." In *O. Henry Memorial Award; Prize Stories of 1932,*
    edited by Blanche Colton Williams. Garden City, N.Y.: Doubleday,
    Doran & Co., 1932.
"Darkness." In *The Best Short Stories of 1921 and Yearbook of the American Short
    Story,* edited by Edward J. O'Brien. Boston: Small, Maynard Co., 1922.
"Faith, Hope, and Charity." In *New Stories for Men,* edited by Charles Grayson.
    Garden City, N.Y.: Doubleday, Doran & Co., 1941.
"Fishhead." In *Beware After Dark!,* edited by Thomas Everett Harre. New
    York: Macaulay Co., 1929.
"The Great Auk." In *The Best Short Stories of 1916 and Yearbook of the American
    Short Story,* edited by Edward J. O'Brien. Boston: Small, Maynard & Co.,
    1917.
"Irvin S. Cobb and 'The Escape of Mr. Trimm.'" In *My Maiden Effort,* edited,
    with introduction, by Gelett Burgess. Garden City, N.Y.: Doubleday,
    Page & Co., 1921.
"A Little Town Called Montignies St. Christophe." In *The Saturday Evening
    Post Treasury,* edited by Roger Butterfield et al. New York: Simon &
    Schuster, 1954.

"The Lost Tribes of the Irish in the South." In *World's Great Speeches,* edited by L. Copeland. Garden City, N.Y.: Garden City Publishing Co., 1942.

"Foreword to 'The Escape of Mr. Trimm.'" In *My Story That I Like Best,* edited, with introduction, by Ray Long. New York: International Magazine Co., 1925.

"Snake Doctor." In *First Prize Stories 1919–1960,* edited from the O. Henry Memorial Awards. Garden City, N.Y.: Hanover House, 1960.

"Speaking of Operations." In *The Saturday Evening Post Treasury,* edited by Roger Butterfield et al. New York: Simon & Schuster, 1954.

"A Woman Tells." In *Star Reporters and 34 of Their Stories,* edited by Ward Greene. New York: Random House, 1948.

"Words and Music." In *Stories of the Old South, Old and New,* edited by Addison Hibbard. Chapel Hill: University of North Carolina Press, 1931.

"You Have Ruined My Wife." In *A Treasury of Great Reporting,* edited by Louis L. Snyder and Richard B. Morris. New York: Simon & Schuster, 1949.

4. Articles and Stories in Periodicals

"Accustomed as I Am." *American Magazine* 115 (May 1933):43, 132–33.

"The Advantages of Being Homely." *American Magazine* 86 (July 1918):43–45.

"Answering Mr. F. S. Key." *American Magazine* 90 (September 1920):54–55.

"Arnold Bennett." *American Magazine* 75 (November 1912):36–38.

"At the Feet of the Enemy." *Golden Book* 21 (February 1935):150–54.

"The Bear That Hunted Me." *Cosmopolitan,* March 1922.

"Big Moments of Big Trials." *McClure's Magazine* 46 (November 1915):15–17.

"The Bull Named Emily." *Golden Book* 2 (November 1925):663–70.

"Cabbages and Kings." *Good Housekeeping* 91 (July 1930):68–71.

"The Cater-Cornered Sex." *Saturday Evening Post* 194 (24 September 1921):8–10.

"Chivalry Peak." *Good Housekeeping* 84 (May 1927):22–26, (June 1927):30–33; 85 (July 1927):74–78, (August 1927):88–91.

"The Coyote in Central Park." *Good Housekeeping* 81 (July 1925):22–26.

"Darkness." *Saturday Evening Post* 194 (20 August 1921):3–5.

"Dearest Word." *American Magazine* 91 (April 1921):45.

"The Eminent Dr. Deeves." *Current Opinion* 74 (June 1923):692–701.

"The Exit of Anse Dugmore." *Saturday Evening Post,* December 1910.

"Fellow Travelers." *Saturday Evening Post* 193 (2 October 1920):6.

"Flirtation, Ltd." *Good Housekeeping* 93 (2 October 1931):20–21.

"The Funniest Thing That Ever Happened to Me." *American Magazine* 96 (October 1923):24–25.

"The Generation That's Next." *Saturday Evening Post* 194 (17 September 1921):6–7.

"George Horace Lorimer, Original Easy Boss." *Bookman* 48 (December 1918):389–94.

"Glory of the States; Kentucky." *American Magazine* 81 (May 1916):19–20.

"The Great Reduction!" *Saturday Evening Post* 194 (16 July 1921):3–4.

"The Greatest Thrill I Ever Had." *American Magazine* 90 (December 1920):54–55.

"His Mother's Apron Strings." *Good Housekeeping* 75 (March 1923):10–13.

"How to Begin at the Top and Work Down." *American Magazine* 100 (August 1925):34–35.

"I Admit I Am a Good Reporter." *American Magazine* 88 (August 1919):60–61.

"I Am Strangely Moved by the Movies!" *Woman's Home Companion* 44 (July 1917):15.

"Inside Stories." *Saturday Evening Post* 93 (10 July 1920):3–4.

"In the Nature of a Preliminary Announcement." *Saturday Evening Post* 93 (8 January 1921):8–9.

"J. Poindexter, Colored." *Saturday Evening Post* 194 (10 June 1922):12–13; (17 June 1922):24–28; (24 June 1922):18–19; (1 July 1922):20–21.

"Killed with Kindness." *Golden Book* 14 (August 1931):51–60.

"Kipling Interviewed at Last." *Literary Digest* 47 (27 December 1913):1277.

"A Letter to a Relative." *Good Housekeeping* 76 (November 1923):10–11.

"The Long Pants Age." *Good Housekeeping* 81 (August 1925):30–33.

"Looking Both Ways from Forty." *American Magazine* 83 (May 1917):11–14.

"Miste-er Chairma-an!" *Saturday Evening Post* 192 (5 June 1920):3–4.

"My Free Recipe for Getting Rich." *Rotarian* 43 (September 1933):11–13.

"The Nearest I Ever Came to Death." *American Magazine* 94 (December 1922):5–7.

"No Dam' Yankee." *Golden Book* 15 (April 1932):316–28.

"Nothing to Write About." *Good Housekeeping* 93 (August 1931):48–49.

"O! O! McIntyre?" *Delineator* 124 (March 1934):4.

"Oh, Well, You Know How Women Are!" *American Magazine* 88 (October 1919):10–11.

"Old Ben Alibi." *Golden Book* 17 (March 1933):193–209.

"One Block from Fifth Avenue." *Golden Book* 1 (May 1925):629–40.

"One-third Off." *Saturday Evening Post* 194 (23 July 1921):6–7.

"A Plea for Old Cap Collier." *Saturday Evening Post* 193 (3 July 1920):3–4.

"A Plea in Abatement of Pants." *American Magazine* 87 (March 1919):48–49.

"The Plural of Moose is Mise." *Field and Stream* 75 (March 1981):99–103.

"A Quest in Youbetcherland." *Saturday Evening Post* 193 (1 January 1921):6–7.

"The Ravelin' Wolf." *Saturday Evening Post* 192 (21 February 1920):12–13.

"A Short Natural History." *Saturday Evening Post* 193 (9 October 1920):3–5.

"Snake Doctor." *Cosmopolitan* 46 (November 1922).

"Speaking of Operations." *Saturday Evening Post* 46 (6 November 1915).

"The Story That Ends Twice." *Saturday Evening Post* 193 (4 September 1920):8–10.
"The Strange Adventures of the Man Who Wrote a Play." *Munsey's Magazine,* November 1908, 20–25.
"The Taste of Freedom." *Pictorial Review* 35 (November 1933):12–13.
"That Shall He Also Reap." *Saturday Evening Post* 195 (15 July 1922):16–17.
"This Thing Called Luck." *Pictorial Review* 36 (January 1935):22–23.
"Three Good Men." *Publisher's Weekly,* 145 (18 March 1944):1225.
"The Three Wise Men of the East Side." *Golden Book* 11 (February 1930):54–61.
"The Trail of the Lonesome Laugh." *Everybody's Magazine* 24 (April 1911):467–75.
"Trial and Error." *Reader's Digest* 41 (December 1942):32.
"Two of Everything." *Golden Book* 16 (October 1932):289–302.
"The Undoing of Stonewall Jackson Bugg." *McClure's Magazine* 45 (September 1915):38–39.
"The Wasted Headline." *Saturday Evening Post* 192 (8 May 1920):10–11.
"Whither Are We Thrifting." *Saturday Evening Post* 192 (12 June 1920):10–11.
"Who's Who at the Zoo?" *Hampton Magazine* 27 (October 1911):421–30.
"Why Are Women Like That?" *American Magazine* 115 (April 1933):56–57.
"Why Mr. Lobel Had Apoplexy." *Saturday Evening Post* 192 (17 January 1920):8–9.
"The Widow Arrives." *American Magazine* 132 (August 1936):32–35.
"Worth $10,000!" *Saturday Evening Post* 194 (24 December 1921):12–13.

SECONDARY SOURCES

This bibliography contains a few selected reviews. Complete bibliographic information upon other reviews can be found in the notes.

1. Books

Banta, R. E. *The Ohio.* Rivers of America Series. New York: Rinehart & Company, 1949. A historical study of the Ohio River. Useful as a gloss to Cobb's *All Aboard.* Says that "modern Paducah rode to fame on the white linen coattails of Irvin S. Cobb" (555).
Bennett, Arnold. *Your United States: Impressions of a First Visit.* New York: Harper and Brothers, 1912. An eminent British novelist visits the Cobbs and sees America through the eyes of young Elisabeth Cobb.
Burkhalter, Betty L. "A Rhetorical Study of Irvin S. Cobb" M.A. thesis, Murray State University, 1967. An examination of the structure of

Cobb's writings, especially his speeches, according to the principles of Aristotelian rhetoric.

Carson, Gerald. *The Social History of Bourbon.* New York: Dodd, Mead & Co., 1963. An entertaining and informative history that repeatedly mentions Cobb and his novel *Red Likker.* Useful both for Cobb biography and for the historical context of *Red Likker* as well as of many Judge Priest stories.

Case, Frank. *Tales of a Wayward Inn.* New York: Frederick A. Stokes Co., 1938. Contains several Cobb anecdotes, particularly one about Cobb's election to the Advisory Board of the Chemical Bank and Trust Company.

Davis, Robert H. *Irvin S. Cobb, Storyteller: With Biographical Particulars and Notes on His Books and Who's Cobb and Why?* New York: George H. Doran Co., n.d. [1924?]. *Who's Cobb and Why?* is a reprint of an article by Davis in the *New York Sun.* It is an admiring short biography of Cobb. Contains also reprint of Butler's "Mr. Cobb of Paducah" from *Obiter Dictum.* Excellent material on the nature of Cobb's humor. Lillian Bell's "The Books of Irvin Cobb," from *Book Talk and Things,* offers useful comments about Cobb's "depersonalized" humor and his use of pathos.

————.*Canada Cavalcade: The Maple Leaf Dominion from Atlantic to Pacific.* New York: D. Appleton-Century Co., 1937. Recollects the first season Cobb spent fishing at Ojuk Island, when he planned a series of short stories, some of them Judge Priest tales.

————.*Over My Left Shoulder.* New York: D. Appleton & Co., 1926. Chapter 40, "I Find Pitfalls in Playing Boswell to Irvin Cobb," is an amusing anecdote about Cobb's school days.

Doran, George H. *Chronicles of Barabbas.* New York: Rinehart & Co., 1952. Cobb's principal book publisher recalls Cobb's rise to fame from the time in 1909 when the backyard of the Doran house in Westchester overlooked that of the Cobbs.

Hall, Wade. *The Smiling Phoenix: Southern Humor from 1865 to 1914.* Gainsville, Fla.: University of Florida Press, 1965. Contends that Cobb did not write "Southern" humor.

Hohenberg, John. *Foreign Correspondents: The Great Reporters and Their Times.* New York: Columbia University Press, 1964. An account of the activities of Cobb and other correspondents who covered the invasion of Brussels by the German army in August 1914.

Jillson, Willard Rouse. *Irvin S. Cobb at Frankfort, Kentucky.* Carrollton, Ky.: News-Democrat Press, 1944. A thorough and intimate account of Cobb's activities in Frankfort during the time when he covered the Goebel trial.

Kahn, E. J., Jr. *The World of Swope.* New York: Simon & Schuster, 1965. Account of Swope's interview with Kipling and of Kipling's reaction to Cobb's reporting techniques.

Lawson, Anita. *Irvin S. Cobb.* Bowling Green, Ohio: Bowling Green University Press, 1984. To date, the most thorough and objective biographical study of Cobb. Especially thorough on Cobb's work in motion pictures and on his Hollywood years in general.

Long, Ray. *20 Best Short Stories in Ray Long's 20 years as Editor.* New York: Ray Long & Richard R. Smith, 1932. In a section titled "A Regular 'Regular,'" Cobb's *Cosmopolitan* editor includes Cobb's story "Snake Doctor" and tells of the origin and writing of the story.

Masson, Thomas L. *Our American Humorists.* New York: Moffat, Yard & Co., 1922. A section titled "Irvin Cobb" is a review of Cobb's life and work. It seeks to diminish Mencken's adverse remarks upon Cobb and praises Cobb's humor as "impersonal."

Mathews, Joseph J. *Reporting the Wars.* Minneapolis: University of Minneapolis Press, 1957. Assesses Cobb's place among the great war correspondents. Compares him with his contemporary Richard Harding Davis.

Mencken, H. L. *Prejudices: First Series.* New York: Alfred A. Knopf, 1919. In a chapter titled "The Heir of Mark Twain" Mencken denies that Cobb should be considered Twain's literary heir and quotes Cobb's works to show that Cobb's humor is seriously overvalued by the American reading public.

Mott, Frank Luther. *American Journalism: A History 1690–1960.* 3d ed. New York: Macmillan Co., 1962. Retells and assesses the war correspondence Cobb wrote for the *Saturday Evening Post.*

Neuman, Fred G. *Irvin S. Cobb: His Life and Letters.* Introduction by O. O. McIntyre. Emaus, Pa.: Rodale Press, 1938. The first full-scale biography of Cobb. Lacks last six years of life. Written by a Paducah newspaperman and good friend of Cobb. Encyclopedic chronological presentation of facts. A large number of anecdotes about Cobb.

————.*The Story of Irvin S. Cobb: A Sketch of His Life and Achievements.* Paducah, Ky.: Young Printing Co., 1926. A "concise" early biography of Cobb, later expanded into full version.

————.*The Story of Paducah (Kentucky).* Paducah, Ky.: Young Printing Co., 1927. General history of Paducah, with a considerable section on the life of Cobb as a Paducah native.

Overton, Grant Martin. *When Winter Comes to Main Street.* New York: George H. Doran Co., 1922. Section titled "Cobb's Fourth Dimension" is devoted mostly to examination of *J. Poindexter, Colored* and *Stickfuls.* Contains long quotations from Robert H. Davis, editor of *Munsey's.*

Pattee, Fred Lewis. *The New American Literature, 1890–1930.* New York: Cooper Square Publishers, 1968. Compares Cobb with Richard Harding Davis as newspaperman and identifies Cobb as one of many "non-New England" writers of his era and a derivative of the "O. Henry school."

Piercy, Josephine K., ed. *Modern Writers at Work.* New York: Macmillan

Co., 1931. Cobb argues that the only way to learn to write the English language is to work, practice, and study—no short cuts.

Ross, Ishbel. *Ladies of the Press: The Story of Women in Journalism.* New York: Harper & Brothers, 1936. Tells of the four female reporters covering the Thaw trial with Cobb. At this time women reporters were called "sob sisters" by newspeople.

Shepherd, Jean, ed. *The America of George Ade.* New York: Capricorn Books, 1961. Shepherd's introduction is a useful short essay upon the development of American humor.

Tebbel, John. *The American Magazine: A Compact History.* New York: Hawthorn Books, 1969. Characterizes Cobb, among others, as a principal contributor to *McClure's* and the *Saturday Evening Post.*

————. *The Compact History of the American Newspaper.* New York: Hawthorn Books, 1963. Has a good short description of "Hard-Boiled Charlie" Chapin, Cobb's *New York World* editor. Gives one version of the story about Cobb's famous quip upon hearing of Chapin's illness.

Townsend, John Wilson. *Kentucky in American Letters.* Vol. 2. Cedar Rapids, Iowa: Torch Press, 1913. Has a good if overenthusiastic summary of Cobb's career to 1912.

————. *Irvin S. Cobb.* Library of Southern Literature, vol. 17. Atlanta: Martin & Hoyt Co., 1923. Has a good chronology of Cobb's life and works to 1923, along with a short bibliography.

Williams, Blanche Colton. *Our Short Story Writers.* New York: Dodd, Mead & Co., 1920. Contains a brief biography of Cobb to 1920.

Wood, James Playsted. *The Curtis Magazines.* New York: Ronald Press Co., 1971. Contains a comprehensive section on George Horace Lorimer, including Cobb as a member of the "SatEvePost school of writers."

Van Gelder, Robert. *Writers and Writing.* New York: Charles Scribner's Sons, 1946. Contains a useful section titled "Irvin S. Cobb Discusses His Writing" (232–36). Cobb discloses his attitudes toward and ideas upon humor, hard work, fiction, and newswriting. He provides an estimate of himself as a writer of fiction, and he tells about how he wrote *Exit Laughing.*

Yates, Morris Wilson. *The American Humorist: Conscience of the Twentieth Century.* Ames: Iowa State University Press, 1964. Chapter entitled "The Crackerbarrel Sage in the West and South: Will Rogers and Irvin S. Cobb" is an indispensable examination of the nature of Cobb's humor. Unlike Rogers, Cobb was a "yarnspinner" but nonetheless in the mainstream of the humor of his time.

2. Articles

"American Humorists: Irvin S. Cobb." *Journal of the National Education Association* 14 (March 1925):101. English critics contend that Cobb is America's best short story writer.

"American Readers Will Miss Them." *Senior Scholastic* 44 (1 May 1944):22. Discusses Cobb as both humorist and human being.

"An Attempt to Place Irvin S. Cobb Among the Immortals." *Current Opinion* 54 (January 1913):56. Discusses Robert H. Davis's opinion that Cobb is one of America's great writers, and reasons why.

Angly, Edward. "What's the Matter With the United States?" *New York Herald,* 8 May 1932, 20. Reports Cobb's opinions upon America's short-comings in society, politics, and international affairs. Condemns prohibition as a failure.

Benét, William Rose. "Mortality in Writers." *Saturday Review of Literature* 27 (18 March 1944):14. A useful overview of Cobb's life and certain of his writings. Praises "Fishhead" as a "macabre classic."

Bruner, Margaret E. "In Thoughtful Mood." *News-Republican* (New Cortes, Indiana), 21 June 1963, p. 3. Examines Cobb as humorist, dramatist, story writer, and newsman. Speculates upon how Cobb probably felt about his black friends as people.

Campbell, Sara Smith. "The Clown Prince of Gourmets." *Louisville Courier-Journal,* Sunday magazine sec., undated clipping. Illuminates Cobb's love of good "back-home" cooking.

————. "Master of the Word." *Louisville Courier-Journal,* Sunday magazine sec., undated clipping. Particularly useful information upon Cobb's early years, especially the location of the family home.

"Censorship or Not." *Literary Digest* 87 (23 June 1923):27–29. Quotes a portion of a letter from Cobb, who condemns overstrict censorship but urges writers to be responsible.

Clemens, Cyril. "A Chat With Irvin S. Cobb." *Hobbies—The Magazine for Collectors* 44 (August 1944):99–101. Influence of Twain and others on Cobb.

"Concerning Irvin Cobb." *Bookman* 37 (March 1913):14–15. Quotes heavily from Davis's *Who's Cobb and Why?* in order to demonstrate the excessive level of enthusiasm for Cobb. Registers skepticism about that enthusiasm but admits that Cobb's future looks bright.

Davis, Robert H. "Introducing Mr. Cobb." *Golden Book Magazine* 19 (January 1934):17–17a. A "brief biographical note" in which Davis despairs of telling a story that Cobb has not already heard. Pays tribute to Cobb's broad general knowledge. Cobb is guest editor.

————. "Irvin S. Cobb, Hunter, Angler and Dreamer." *Field and Stream* 33 (December 1928):11–13, 81, 86.

"Death Comes to Famous Paducah Humorist After 3 Months Illness." *Paducah Sun-Democrat,* undated clipping. Contains four articles on Cobb' death, one by Fred Neuman, Cobb's biographer.

"Exit Laughing." *Newsweek* 23 (20 March 1944):98. Contains a good capsule of Cobb's New York newspaper work.

Fowler, Clarence. "The Gardens at 'Rebel Ridge,' Home of Irvin S. Cobb,

Westchester County, N.Y." *Garden Magazine* 34 (December 1921):203–
4. A description of the Cobb estate three miles from Ossining, New
York.

"Fox Has Smash Hit With Rogers in 'Judge Priest.'" *Hollywood Reporter,* 3
August 1934, 3. "Trade paper" review of Judge Priest movie.

Gordon, Sloane. "The Story of Irvin S. Cobb." *Pearson's Magazine* 33 (March
1915):278–84. Predicts a bright future for Cobb. Examines his
strengths, weakness, and successes.

"Hal Corbett Springs a New One on Irvin S. Cobb at N.Y. Banquet." *Paducah
News-Democrat,* undated clipping (ca. 1916). Reprint of a speech by Hal
Corbett at the Kentucky Club. He speaks flatteringly of Cobb's talent
and modesty.

Henderson, Alma E. "Irvin S. Cobb." *American Author,* November 1932,
11–12. Useful summary of Cobb's memberships, appointments, degrees,
and other honors. Compares Cobb favorably with other famous authors.

Henderson, Kathleen H. "Judge William Sutton Bishop." *Advance-Yeoman*
(Wickliffe, Kentucky), 7 September 1972, pp. 1–3. Contains the most
complete information upon Judge Bishop, Cobb's model for Judge
Priest.

"His Pen Made Paducah Famous." *Illinois Central Magazine,* July 1940. An
enthusiastic review of Neuman's biography of Cobb.

"A Humorist and His Wrist-Watch." *Literary Digest* 53 (12 August
1916):378–79. An illuminating incident in which Cobb affronted oldtime Southerners by wearing a wrist watch during a speech he delivered.

"Irvin Cobb Builds Himself a House." *House and Garden* 41 (February
1922):26–27. An architectural evaluation of the ingenuity with which
Cobb used native materials in building his Westchester home.

"Irvin Cobb Greeted at Waldorf Dinner." *New York Times,* 25 April 1915, p.
7. Cobb is guest of honor at a dinner for 700 persons who nominate him
to succeed William Jennings Bryan as official Fourth of July orator.

"Irvin Cobb—Our Leading Literary Heavyweight." *Current Opinion* 74 (February 1923):231–32. A poll of ten prominent literati gives Cobb "a kind
of primacy in American letters." Also provides two sample anecdotes
from Cobb's current column in the *New York Sun.*

"Irvin S. Cobb Proves That Humorists Are Able to Buy Food." *Literary Digest*
62 (19 July 1919):58–60. Cobb explains how he can laugh at himself
and make money at his own expense. A useful discussion of the psychology of humor in the craft of writing.

Ives, Marguerite. "Some Noted Outdoorsmen I Have Met—Irvin S. Cobb."
Outdoor Recreation 73 (July 1925):36–37, 81–82. A noted writer about
outdoorsmen includes Cobb in her series of articles. Cobb explains his
lifelong fascination with birds and says that he feels so intensely about
the outdoors that he refuses to write about it for money.

Jackson, Edward N. "How Famous Men and Women Face the Camera."

American Magazine 93 (February 1922):44–47. A "celebrity photographer" psychoanalyzes Cobb and other celebrities by how they face a camera.

Kieft, Alice Clark. "Man From Paducah." *Christian Science Monitor,* 13 May 1944, p. 6. A report of an interview with Cobb. Wide range of subjects.

Knight, Grant C. "Bluegrass and Laurel; The Varieties of Kentucky Fiction." *Saturday Review of Literature* 28 (6 January 1945): 12–13. Cobb's character Judge Priest is compared with David Harum and Eben Holder, other fictional characters of a similar kind.

"Large Footprints: Hon. William S. Bishop 'Old Judge Priest.'" In *Paducah, 100 Years of Progress.* Paducah, Ky.: City of Paducah, 1976. This centennial celebration booklet contains extraordinary information about Judge Bishop as the model for the fictional Judge Priest.

Lowry, Helen Bullitt. "If You Have Talent." *Good Housekeeping* 80 (February 1925):42. Cobb argues that newspaper work is the best means of discovering writing talent in oneself.

Marquis, Don. "Confessions of a Reformed Columnist." *Saturday Evening Post* 201 (29 December 1928):59–60. A noted humorist observes that most "good things" in contemporary columns are said to be Cobb's.

Maurice, Arthur Bartlett. "The History of Their Books. VII. Irvin S. Cobb." *Bookman* 69 (July 1929):511–14. Details the backgrounds of stories, novels, and best-known characters created by Cobb.

"Paducah Saves Market House and Gains Cultural Center." *Louisville Courier-Journal,* "Today's Living Section," 25 February 1972, p. A16. An account of the restoration of the historic Market House closely associated with Cobb's boyhood in Paducah. Contains mementos of native sons Irvin Cobb and Alben Barkley.

Melcher, Frederic G. "Three Good Men," *Publishers' Weekly,* 18 March 1944, 1201. Obituary article upon the recent deaths of Cobb, Joseph Lincoln, and Hendrick Willem Van Loon. Brief but useful comments upon Judge Priest and Cobb's quips.

"Much Better." *Newsweek* 22 (20 December 1943):70. Cobb promises to let his friends know if and when he plans to "depart elsewhere." His death had just been erroneously reported.

O'Brien, Edward J. "The Best Sixty-Three American Short Stories of 1917." *Bookman* 46 (February 1918):696–706. Gives reasons why O'Brien rates Cobb's three stories "Boys Will Be Boys," "The Family Tree," and "Quality Folks" as numbers 13, 14, and 15 out of the sixty-three best short stories of 1917.

"Old Judge Priest Treads the Boards." *New York Times,* 16 November 1916, p. 6. Review of the stage version of the Judge Priest stories called "Back Home." Says the play is "mild and rambling" but "rich in tenderness and humor."

Overton, Grant. "Irvin S. Cobb: Ask Him Another." *Bookman* 65 (August

1927):673–77. A comprehensive and useful discussion of Cobb as "an ambling short story writer" and as a humorist.

Paulding, G. C. "On All Fours." *Commonweal* 39 (24 December 1943):245–46. Reminds readers that the witty Irvin Cobb is still alive and well as of December 1943, at age sixty-seven.

"Politics on the Cobb." *Nation* 111 (17 July 1920):62–63. Effusive, tongue-in-cheek report of a 1920 presidential nominating convention. Contends that Cobb would have taken more votes than Harding.

Powell, Bill. "Kettler House Was Birthplace of Irvin Cobb." *Advance-Yeoman* (Wickliffe, Kentucky), 22 May 1963. Provides evidence that Kettler's Boarding House was Cobb's birthplace.

"Paducah Shrine." *Hobbies* 58 (December 1953):44. Discusses Paducah as source and background for the humor and local color in Cobb's work.

Paxton, E. G., ed. "Irvin S. Cobb: He'd Be 100 Today." *Paducah Sun-Democrat,* 23 June 1976, p. 4A. A highly complimentary discussion of Cobb's social and racial attitudes, with an overview of his writing career.

Pendennis. "'My Types'—Irvin S. Cobb." *Forum* 58 (October 1917):471–80. A long and useful interview with Cobb, preceded by an introduction to that author. Cobb discusses his theories of humor and fiction writing, saying that style is a matter of good taste and that faith in human nature is a necessary attitude for a writer.

"Portrait." *Time* 34 (21 August 1939):29. A report of Cobb's hospitalization for a stomach ailment in San Francisco. Good biographical locus.

Rice, Grantland. "Fin Ahead!" *Collier's* 80 (24 September 1927):30. A famous sports writer describes a swordfishing expedition off Montauk point. This was Cobb's first experience with catching swordfish.

Sanderson, Bob, ed. "Irvin S. Cobb"; "Hash Headline Sent Cobb Back to a Beat"; "A Slow Start, A Big Ending." *Paducah Sun-Democrat,* undated clipping. A useful collection of magazine articles printed together on a single page of the Paducah newspaper.

Serling, Rod. "Tonight's American . . . Irvin S. Cobb." *Our America,* 7 October 1951. A sustaining national radio broadcast on WLW–T. A radio script in the Cobb collection at the Paducah Public Library.

Smith, Donald B. "The Legend of Chief Buffalo Child Long Lance and the Mysterious Truth Behind It." *Canadian* (magazine section of the *Toronto Star*), 7 February 1976, 13–18. Part 1 of a two-part article explaining that Cobb's close friend Buffalo Child Long Lance was neither a chief nor an Indian.

————. "Long Lance's Last Stand, Dying is a Lie." *Canadian* (magazine section of the *Toronto Star*), 14 February 1976, 10–13. Conclusion of the foregoing article. An astounding and regrettable development in the life of a man whom Cobb greatly admired.

Stuart, Henry L. "Irvin S. Cobb." *Book News Monthly,* February 1914, 261–

67. Compares Cobb favorably with Poe and Hawthorne as a writer of the eerie and the bizarre.

"They Spin Yarns to Please You." *Collier's* 58 (18 November 1916):12–13. Portraits and capsule descriptions of some of the best-known writers of the time, including Cobb and Kathleen Norris.

"Tom Waller's Tribute to Irvin Shrewsbury Cobb." *Paducah News-Democrat,* 8 October 1944. Prints the text of Tom Waller's funeral sermon for his old friend Irvin Cobb.

"25 Years Pass . . . 'To Whom It May Concern.'" *Paducah Sun-Democrat,* 10 March 1968, pp. 5–7. A reprinting of Cobb's famous "death-bed letter," reprinted here twenty-five years after the author's death.

Index